Being OK
with
Not Being OK

Being OK with Not Being OK

Embracing God's Design for You – and Everyone You Know (and Don't Know)

Clyde L. Pilkington, Jr.

BIBLE STUDENT'S PRESS ™
Windber, Pennsylvania

Being OK with Not Being OK – *Embracing God's Design for You – and Everyone You Know (and Don't Know)*
by Clyde L. Pilkington, Jr.
Copyright © 2012 by Clyde L. Pilkington, Jr.
All rights reserved.

Original Printing:
   Individual articles published in the *Bible Student's Notebook,*
   ©1989-2012

Second Printing::
   First book edition, 2012

Executive Editor: André Sneidar
Associate Editors: Richard Lemons; Nadine Sneidar
Layout and Design: Great Adventure in Faith

Cover design by Clyde L. Pilkington, III
   Photograph: © Can Stock Photo Inc. / oly5

   ISBN-10:   1-934251-90-9
   ISBN-13:   978-1-934251-90-4

Published by
   Bible Student's Press™
   An imprint of *Pilkington & Sons*
   P.O. Box 265
   Windber, PA 15963

For other titles by the author, visit
   www.ClydePilkington.com

For information on *Bible Student's Press*™ releases, visit
   www.BibleStudentsPress.com

For information on other Bible study resources, visits
   www.StudyShelf.com

Printed in the United States of America.

Everything will be okay in the end. If it's not okay, then it's not the end.

Contents

1. You're Not OK 11

About You

2. "Shoulda," "Coulda," "Woulda" 19
3. Your Uniqueness 23
4. Tailor-Made Trials 29
5. Lessons from Your Weaknesses 31
6. Life's Not Over 35
7. "God Meant It for Good" 41
8. "I Create Evil" 43
9. "Shall We Not Receive Evil?" 45
10. "Though He Slay Me" 47
11. "But if Not" 49
12. "Nevertheless" 53
13. You're His Masterpiece 59
14. He Will Finish What He Started 61
15. A Complaining Spirit 63
16. Giving Father Thanks for All Things 67
17. Real Life 69
18. Real Worship 73
19. Mornings and Evenings 75

About Others

20. Seeing Others as Father Does 81
21. Trusting Others to Father 85
22. Give Yourself and Others Some Slack 89
23. Don't Let Them Agitate You! 91

About God

24. All of Your Days Were Written in His Book 97
25. Stages of Life 99
26. The Long Process of Growth 101
27. Just How Much God Is Your God? 105
28. The Contrasts of Life 107
29. "All Things Are of God" 113
30. "All Things Work Together" 117
31. The Potter Has the Power 119

The Conclusion of the Whole Matter

32. Being OK 129
Postscript: Facts Concerning God and You 125

DEDICATED TO ...

— Those who have been abused at the hands of religion for being what God made them – *human*.

— Those who have struggled with their brokenness, trying to correct it, not knowing that it is currently the Father's wise plan that they be subject to such *frailty*.

— Those who long to be free from themselves and their circumstances, not knowing that true *freedom and rest* is actually to be *found in just what Father has made them* – **as** they are, **where** they are.

Chapter 1

You're Not OK

You just want to be OK. Your struggles are constant; your conflicts are continuous; your battles are endless. You just look forward to that place – that place and time in life – where everything will just finally be OK.

Really though, who in this life truly is OK? The simple fact of the matter is that, regardless of what outward appearances may suggest, we *all* are weak, frail, flawed and endlessly faltering creatures – all of us, *without exception*. The entire creation – every last bit of it – has been subjected, against their will, to vanity. None can escape it; not even you. This is why Paul, the Apostle wrote,

The creature was made **subject**[1] *to vanity,*[2] *not willingly,*

---
1. The Greek work for *"Made subject"* is rendered *"placed under"* in the *Emphatic Diaglot*.
2. The Greek word translated as *"vanity"* here is *mataiotēs*, and is defined by Joseph Thayer (*Thayer's Greek-English Lexicon of the New Testament*) as: "What is devoid of truth and appropriateness; perverseness, depravity, frailty, want [*i.e.,* lack] of vigor." B.W. Johnson (*People's New Testament*) defines it as "seeking without finding."
It is translated in the following ways by various versions.
  "aimless frustration" (*An Understandable Version*)
  "spoiled" (*Bible in Worldwide English*)

but by reason of Him Who has subjected the same in confident expectation.[3]

This all will be gloriously and permanently corrected in the resurrection, but you might as well go ahead and admit it: currently you're broken, and you aren't going to be "fixed" for now. Granted, you may have some days that are better than others, some circumstances that seem to indicate that you are OK, but the wearisome cycle simply will recur.

Thus it is by design – by divine design. Father is bringing you to a place where you are OK with not being OK, where you simply rest in His current purpose and plan in your training and development for that grand and magnificent culmination that He has so wonderfully and skillfully designed especially for you – in your next life.

THE CHRISTIAN "FIX"

Christianity always wants to "fix" everything. Religious bookstores abound in "How to ..." books. Clergymen continually weary their parishioners with what they must *do* to correct things. The pressure is constantly on to get it all corrected, focusing on the problems, on the circumstances, on changing everything – on deliverance from what makes us not OK. Please don't be influenced to buy into this illusive dream.

Though you may have recurring periods of better circum-

"frustrated" (Goodspeed New Testament)
"imperfection" (Montgomery New Testament)
"folly" (The Riverside New Testament)
"failure and unreality" (Weymouth New Testament)
"futile" (Moffat New Testament)
"weak" (New Life Study Testament)
"imperfection" (Centenary Translation)
"dissolution" (Original New Testament)

3. Romans 8:20.

stances and better performances, that which ultimately stops you from being truly OK will never change in this lifetime. The root of your real problem is not coming from your varied and fluctuating circumstances; they are actually coming from the design of God found in you – the failure to which *He* has subjected you. He has purposefully and expertly created you with flaws – an abundance of them – that will never go away in this lifetime.

Count on it: if God Himself, in His great wisdom and love for you, has – at this time – subjected you to futility, all of the self-help-religion in the world won't be able to change it.

THE REAL ANSWER

Because of this wise and competent plan of Father, the real answer is never to be found in you at all. The answer is to be found in Him – and in Him alone. It is to be found in knowing just Who He really is, and just what His plans are for you in this temporal life. The answer is to be found in Father's abounding grace for you, even in the middle of your most trying of circumstances. Paul himself learned this vital truth.

> [God] *said to me, "My grace is sufficient for you: for My strength is made perfect in weakness." Most gladly therefore will I rather glory in my infirmities, that the power of Christ may rest on me. Therefore I take pleasure in infirmities ... for when I am weak, then am I strong.*[4]

---
4. II Corinthians 12:9-10.

I Am What I Am

By the grace of God I am what I am. — Paul, the Apostle[5]

"*I am what I am.*" Herein lays a *great* key. God has made you what you are. *You* are His handiwork[6] – every bit of you – flaws and all. *You* are what you are by God's direct hand. Rest in Him. Rest in His work in you. Rest in His plan for you. Rest in His sure outcome for you.

We can learn to be thankful even for the sufferings and hardships of this life. In a seemingly strange, yet divine way, we can be thankful even for our bouts with complaining, realizing that they, too, are a godsend. After all, "*all things are of God,*"[7] even the "*evil spirit from the* LORD" that troubled King Saul.[8] For, even for us, our complaining makes us realize that this world is not our home and creates in us such a strong desire for something more, something better – and that better thing is Father Himself!

So, relax; the way you are is His outworking in you.

Being OK with *Others* Not Being OK

It's the same for other people as well: they are who they are. We are all in His skillful hands; each one of us designed and being masterfully crafted to fit into His glorious, creative collage.

Just as it is true that we are the way we are because Father is working in *us,* even so He is working His expert plan per-

---
5. I Corinthians 15:10.
6. "*We are His workmanship*" (Ephesians 2:10, *KJV*).
   "*His achievement are we*" (*CLT*).
   "*We are His handiwork*" (*Weymouth*).
7. II Corinthians 5:18.
8. I Samuel 16:14.

fectly and precisely in *all* of His creation, as He is the *"faithful Creator."*[9]

Father is extremely good at His job, and just as with any other work, you can't judge the finished product when seeing it in some stage of its development. This is true of you and me, but it is also true of our loved ones and friends – *all of God's creation!*

Attempting to be "God" to someone is an especially hard job if you are not qualified. There is only One in the universe qualified for such a daunting task, and He already has all things squarely under His control.

Don't be discouraged when you look around you. What you see is not the end of God's plan and purpose. What you see is not the finished product of God. God is actively at work in us in every circumstance, of every life. He is steadily and successfully working *"everything by the intention of His Own will,"* finding no challenge with the circumstances and lives of our loved ones – not even the hard cases. Nothing poses an obstacle to Him – after all, He *is* the *Almighty* God.

Don't be overwhelmed: you're not the Workman. God is. He's the One in charge. He loves others just as unconditionally as He loves you. He is molding them as surely as He is you – day-by-day – into *all* that He intends for them to be, regardless of what we may think we currently see.

One day you'll be OK. In the resurrection Father will perfect His work in you. Until then you can be OK with not being OK. It's all Father's plan. To Him, beautiful is the mess we are.

So, relax and enjoy *His* work.

---
9. I Peter 4:19.

About You

Chapter 2

"Shoulda," "Coulda," "Woulda"

Forgetting those things which are behind, and reaching forth to those things which are before; I press toward the mark for the prize of the high calling of God in Christ Jesus —
Paul, the Apostle[1]

We unnecessarily live with the regrets of the past. We think that if we could *just* go back and do things over again, we would do them so differently, and that they would turn out better.

We call this "hindsight," and we always rate it "20/20."

Hindsight is defined as:

> The recognition of the realities, possibilities, or requirements of a situation, event, decision etc., after its occurrence. — *Farlex*

> The opportunity to judge or understand past events using knowledge that you have gained since then. — *MacMillan*

---
1. Philippians 3:13.

This hindsight is simply the wisdom gained by experience. Experience teaches us that if we had to face similar circumstance TODAY, we would do them differently – and why not? Isn't that the *purpose* of experience, to make us wiser?

Regret, however, is defined as:

> A feeling of sadness about something sad or wrong or about a mistake that you have made, and a wish that it could have been different and better. — *Cambridge*

Rather than operating in the wisdom of experience, sometimes we unnecessarily wallow in the regret of the past. Melancholy, and even fits of depression can set in concerning past choices. The plain fact is that we can't go back and change the past. It is impossible; and even if we could actually do so, we would be destined to repeat the same choices that we made on our first go-round. Let me illustrate.

Let's say that May 20, 1967, I received a "U" for "unsatisfactory" on my elementary class math test. Theoretically I *could* live in regret about that test result even to this day. I could think to myself, "If only I could go back and take that test again, I could get an 'S' for 'satisfactory'! In fact, truth be known, I could get all the answers correct – with flying colors! If only I just had it to do all over again."

Well, it may be true that if I had the test to take over again TODAY that it would be a breeze. Why wouldn't it? After all, that was decades ago, and one would think that I would have a lot more practice, experience and knowledge than I did the night of May 19, 1967, as I lay awake over thoughts of my math test the next day.

However, that I could ace that exact same math test is a truth for TODAY, not for May 20, 1967. If I went back to *that* day and took that same test over again, I would get the *exact same results* – no matter how many times I traveled back to that day to retake it. Why would that be? Because if I went back to THAT day in history – I would be at the *exact* same place in my development that I was *then,* with the *exact same* circumstances that were brought to bear on me on *that* day. No matter how many times I could return to that day in my past I would erase all of the intervening days between then and now, and I would make the exact same grade – because there would be *nothing* different in me.

If I went back to May 20, 1967, I would not have the hindsight that I have today. Remember that hindsight is only *"after* the occurrence" and is the experience of "using knowledge that you have gained *since* past events." If I went back in time to take this test I would no longer have the knowledge gained *"after* the occurrence," and could not use any knowledge gained *since* the event. Mistakes of the past are only of value NOW, and only if we have learned from the experience.

Now let's bring God to bear on all of this. He is God, and we are His creation. We are His *"workmanship,"* His *"achievement."*[2] We are not self-made, we are not self-improved; He is our Potter and we are always His clay.[3] At every place and at every stage in our lives we have *always* been right where He wants us; and He uses *everything* around us as His tools to bring us along as His skillfully designed masterpiece.

So, what if you "messed up" in the past? You have always been right where He wants you. It was all a part of His divine plan of *experience.*

---

2. Ephesians 2:10.
3. In Scripture God is spoken of as a Potter, an analogy that places great emphasis on His ever-present hand and well-designed plan in our lives. The Potter always has complete power over His clay. He designs and makes His clay-creation according to His Own masterful plan. He is active in His craftsmanship, with His hands-on skill (see Romans 9:20, 21; *cf.* Isaiah 64:8; Jeremiah 18:1-6).

This is why Paul the Apostle wrote:

> *Tribulation works patience; and patience, experience; and experience, hope: and hope makes not ashamed; because the love of God is shed abroad in our hearts by the Holy Spirit which is given to us.*[4]

Amazing is it not, that God uses our problems (*"tribulation"*) to work in us patience. Then He gives us experience, which brings us hope, or a confident expectation. Then the expectation makes us unashamed, opening the floodgates of God's love pouring out all over our hearts, allowing us to bask in the goodness of His plan for us!

Relax and lighten up about your past; and your present, and your future for that matter. God is God; He is completely in charge. He loves you unconditionally and is molding you – day-by-day – into *all* that He intends for you to be when He is done with you.

Do not be discouraged with His pace, nor with His progress, for He is not yet finished; *but one day,* in the glorious resurrection, you and I will finally be complete – after all, we are His *"workmanship"* and *"achievement"*!

So, now what? Well, in the meantime, enjoy the journey of your lot in life, *knowing that He is at the helm.* You are *right this moment where* He wants you. You are not ahead, nor behind of His schedule. You are spot-on in the divine timetable. Everything is working just as He has planned!

Now, what about all of those past "regrets"? It is time to let them all go. After all, they are a part of *your* past, and *you* belong to Him, so *they* belong to Him, too!

---

[4]. Romans 5:3-5.

Paul, the Apostle, had much in his past for which he could have suffered sleepless nights of remorse. Listen to his important instruction to us:

> *Forgetting those things which are behind, and reaching forth to those things which are before; I press toward the mark for the prize of the high calling of God in Christ Jesus.*[5]

Enjoy the life of God in you!

> *For in Him we live, and move, and have our being.*[6]

---

5. Philippians 3:13-14.
6. Acts 17:28.

Chapter 3

Your Uniqueness

For who makes you to differ from another?
— Paul, the Apostle[1]

You are distinctly unique; Father has created you that way. Don't waste any time attempting to be like anyone else. Refuse to live a life that belongs to someone else. Don't allow yourself to be pushed into a form in which you don't fit – you'll never be able to fill the shoes of another.

Don't be pressured by others to be who they think you should be. Don't be conformed into who they want you to be. You're that unique self that God has made you to be.

Father's Unique Expression

Every life is a unique expression of God. You are no exception. Your life is a part of the divine drama that is displayed on the stage of human history. Though unfinished, it is developing to tell a grand love story.

You do not know today all that Father will fully make of you; but you can trust Him, for He has a definite goal in sight. All of His designs have a distinct plan, and you are a part of it all. Day by day He is slowly and steadily manifesting His

---
1. I Corinthians 4:7.

Own life in you, revealing the unique person that He alone has created you to be.

Reject Uniformity

There are groups that would often have you think, talk, dress, believe and behave just like them. Yet, you are free from all of this. You needn't have to "play the part." It is a part for which you are not adapted to play.

Look at the vast array of God's nature, as examples of God's unique design and particular expression of His handiwork. For example, Father makes no two snowflakes alike, and yet each one is genuine, with its own matchless perfection and beauty. Neither are any two fingerprints the same: they are each authentic, with specific identity. So God has made you the individual that you are, and has given you unique flaws, struggles and handicaps, as well as unique talents, abilities, ideas and characteristics. Embrace these differences; God is using them in making you distinct. Reject uniformity that attempts to spoil His individual workmanship in you!

The Uniqueness of Your Journey

Being at a different place in your life than those around you doesn't necessarily mean that you are "ahead" or "behind" of, or "worse off" or "better off" than the others. It just means that Father needs to take you on a different (and yet at the same time very similar) path due to the uniqueness of His distinct purpose in your life.

> *There are diversities of operations, but it is the same God Who works all in all.* — Paul, the Apostle[2]

God is active in your life, and in the lives of all of those

---
2. I Corinthians 12:6.

around you. You do not need to live a life filled with care, frustration, discouragement and guilt concerning where our Father has you on your journey. You can, by faith, lay hold of the reality of *His Own* unique and personal workmanship in your life. Rest in *His* great workmanship. Be content with what *He* is accomplishing.

You did not make yourself. You are the creation of God, and what He started He will finish.

> *Being confident of this very thing, that He Who has begun a good work in you will perform it until the day of Jesus Christ.* — Paul, the Apostle[3]

Rest, look and wait on your Father. Let your *only* expectation be from Him, and you will never be disappointed!

> *My soul, wait ONLY on God; for my expectation is from Him.* — King David[4]

> *But they who wait on the Lord shall renew their strength; they shall mount up with wings as eagles; they shall run, and not be weary; and they shall walk, and not faint.* — Isaiah, the Prophet[5]

BE THE REAL YOU

Don't settle for an imitation. God designed you uniquely different. Don't measure yourself, nor allow yourself to be measured by the lives of others – not your qualities and successes, nor your faults and failures. Paul, the Apostle said that this was unwise.

> *They measuring themselves by themselves, and compar-*

---
3. Philippians 1:6.
4. Psalm 62:5.
5. Isaiah 40:31.

ing themselves among themselves, are not wise.[6]

Don't "play the role"; be the real you. Be comfortable in the skin in which Father has placed you.

Have complete confidence in God, your Father. Your journey is as unique as you are. What He began in you, He will see to its full completion.

He will do it!

---

6. II Corinthians 10:12

Chapter 4

TAILOR-MADE TRIALS

All is of God. — Paul, the Apostle[1]

The steps of a man are ordered by the LORD. — David, the King[2]

So, you're in a rough spot right now? No worries: it is a place especially designed for you by God. Your trial has been tailor-made just for you by the loving hands of your Father. He knows exactly what you need to bring you to the next place in your growth and life. After all, it is He Who has been working steadily on you since day one. For you are *"His workmanship," "His achievement"*;[3] and what He has started He will faithfully finish. We are, therefore,

> *Confident of this very thing, that He Who has begun a good work in you will perform it until the day of Jesus Christ.* — Paul, the Apostle[4]

What a place of rest faith brings us to. We are exactly where God wants us to be – always have been, always will be. The

1. Romans 11:36.
2. Psalm 37:23.
3. Ephesians 2:10.
4. Philippians 1:6.

trial in which you now find yourself has been carefully tailor-made for you. God is continuing the steady development of His molding of your life. He is smart, really smart; He knows all things, and He knows exactly what He is doing; He always has, He always will. He also knows exactly what you need at this moment in your life – far more than what you think you need.

This trial that you endure, as hard as it may appear to be, is not an accident; it is not a mistake; it is not some foreign intrusion into your heart and soul to do you harm, from which Father must deliver you. No, this trial is His masterwork specifically designed to meet your needs. You are His *"good work,"* and He is skillfully employing *"all things"* – the *"good"* as well as the apparent *"evil"* – to bring about His grand purpose in you, resulting in a glorious finish.

Relax. Rest. Thank Him for His wisdom in placing you in this tailor-made trial. Revel in His all-encompassing, never-failing love for and care of you. Remember that *Father knows best.*

Chapter 5

LESSONS FROM YOUR WEAKNESSES

For He knows our frame; He remembers that we are dust. — King David[1]

The world around you looks to and for greatness, prestige, prominence, honor and reputation. You should know however that God uses foolish, weak, base and despised things.[2] It is in abundant weakness and endless frailty[3] that God will teach you valuable lessons in preparation for the great plans that He has designed for you in the next life.

What are some of the more obvious lessons that He will teach you from your weaknesses?

HIS ALL-SUFFICIENT ABILITY

In your weakness He removes all other supposed sources of personal strength. It is all about Him, and not about you.[4] In your weaknesses you can learn that you are God's creature, that He is responsible for you – who you are, and who you

---
1. Psalm 103:14.
2. I Corinthians 1:26-29.
3. II Corinthians 4:7-18.
4. I Corinthians 15:10.

aren't – what abilities you have, and what abilities you don't. He can bring you to the ultimate place where you realize that you are His – just the way you are – that He made you, that you are His handiwork[5] and He is accomplishing His work in you.[6]

Patience

You can also come to realize that God's work in you takes time. You are able to learn patience with yourself, as well as with others. Those around you are God's handiwork as well. What a difference this understanding can make in your life!

The Acceptance of Others

When you see yourself in your weaknesses, and your acceptance by your Heavenly Father just as you are, it becomes the ground on which you can learn to accept others just as they are, too.[7] It also deters you from judging others.[8]

To Deal Graciously with Others

Your own personal weaknesses and shortcomings will enable you to learn the true nature of God's grace. Through the acknowledgement of your own failures you can learn to be gracious with others.[9]

To Forget

You can't "go forward" "in the past." Understanding the way God sees you, you are able to forget the past. Even Paul, Christ's apostle to us, said that he had learned to forget about

---
5. Ephesians 2:8-10.
6. Philippians 1:6; 2:13; 4:13; II Corinthians 12:9.
7. Romans 15:7.
8. Romans 14:10.
9. Ephesians 4:32; Colossians 3:12-13.

the past, and with great confidence in God, look toward the future that our Heavenly Father has in store.[10] Father is preparing you, too, for a wonderful and glorious future.

---

10. Philippians 3:13-14.

Chapter 6

LIFE'S NOT OVER

Does it seem to you that life is over? It is not.

You will get past these very dark and trying days, and brighter times will come. Your heart can find healing.

Allow your Father to wrap you in the arms of His love and grace. His love for you is boundless and unmovable. He knows your heartache and pain, your disappointment and feelings of emptiness, and even betrayal.

FATHER'S WAYS

Sometimes you ask yourself, "Why is this happening to me?"

This is very common, but you must remember that you see things quite differently than your Heavenly Father does; and His ways are certainly not our ways.

> *For my thoughts are not your thoughts, neither are your ways my ways.*[1]

---
1. Isaiah 55:8

You should thank Father that His ways aren't your ways. He knows all, and does all things to perfection, having your ultimate best in view. Would you really want it any other way? Of course not. So, you don't really need to understand all about your circumstances, do you? No, you can simply trust the One Who does.

Father Is Working in Your Life

Paul, the Apostle, says that our trials and hardships are lightweight compared with the heavyweight glory that He has planned for us in the next life.[2] He also says that these problems are actually working for us to that end. We must remember that Father is working busily in our lives. We must lay hold of this important viewpoint.

M.R. DeHaan wrote,

> We can only see the present and the immediate, but Father sees the whole picture of one's life as it will appear when the last stroke of the brush has completed the picture. In this pattern of our lives there are bright spots and dark backgrounds, all of them necessary for the complete portrait. As we pass through the dark experiences of life, we see only that dark piece.
>
> Our experiences resemble a jigsaw puzzle. Here is a black piece that seems to fit nowhere at all. It does not make sense. Here is a little brighter piece. Other sections of the jigsaw puzzle are dark, and some pitch black, and we cry and moan in these black moments; but by-and-by the Master will take all the pieces that look so disconnected to us now and will carefully arrange each piece in its proper place. Then we shall see His completed work – the work of a Master who makes no mistakes.

---
2. II Corinthians 4:17-18

When it is all ready, we shall find that the dark pieces of the puzzle were as important to the completion of the full beauty of the pattern as the bright sections.

Take heart, dear child of Father. *Father makes no mistakes.* He loves you more than you love Him, and even as the child cannot understand ... an earthly father until he reaches maturity, so, too, we cannot understand all now; but someday we shall understand.[3]

THE PURPOSE OF YOUR TRIALS

Father occasionally leads you on a hard and bitter path so that He might perfect His work in you.

Oswald Chambers shares,

> Let the Father put you on His potter's wheel and whirl you as He likes, and as sure as God is God and you are you, you will turn out exactly in accordance with His design. Don't lose heart in the process; all noble things are difficult.
>
> Every time you venture out in the life of faith, you will find something in your common-sense circumstances that flatly contradicts your faith. Common sense is not faith, and faith is not common sense; they stand in the relation of the natural and the spiritual. Can you trust Jesus Christ where your common sense cannot trust Him? Can you venture heroically on Jesus Christ's statements when the facts of your common-sense life shout, "It's a lie?"
>
> On the mount it is easy to say – "Oh, yes, I believe Father can do it;" but you have to come down into the valley and

---

[3]. M.R. DeHaan, M.D. (1891-1965), *Broken Things – Why We Suffer,* pages 104-105.

meet with facts that laugh ironically at the whole of your mount-of-transfiguration belief. Every time my belief is clear to my own mind, I come across something that contradicts it. Let me say I believe Father will supply all my need, and then let me run dry, with no outlook, and see whether I will go through the trial of faith, or whether I will sink back to something lower.

Faith must be tested, because it can be turned into personal possession only through conflict. The final thing is confidence in the Lord Jesus Christ. Believe steadfastly on Him and all you come up against will develop your faith. There is continual testing in the life of faith. Faith is unutterable trust in Father, trust which never dreams that He will not stand by us.[4]

More than Mere Circumstances

The trials, severe as they may be at times, are just *circumstances*. Our English word "circumstance" is a compound word made up of "circum" (around; surrounding) and "stances" (standing). Your circumstances are those things standing around you, those things which surround your daily life.

Remember that the events in your life do not constitute who we are – they are merely the things that surround you. They are, however, more than *mere* circumstances: because Father has ordained them in your life, they are *divine* circumstances. They are divine testings designed to be the pressing of Father's hand to mold you into His grand purpose.

Steve McVey tells us,

> We are so vulnerable to becoming preoccupied with the things that scream for attention. It's so easy to let

---
4. Oswald Chambers (1874-1917), *My Utmost for His Highest*.

our emotions be drained by things, until we feel empty inside. The answer isn't complicated. It is simply to trust Him. That's all you need. When you don't feel Father's presence in the midst of your circumstances, He is there nonetheless, working out the details of your lifestyle in a way that is perfect and beautiful in His sight. One day you will understand the intricate workings of your Father's hand in the details of your life. For now, your only response must be to know, even when you don't feel anything, you must know, that He only acts in ways that are for your good and His glory.

Choose to lean on your Father. Know that at every moment His arms are around you, sustaining you and holding you. That will never change. Though the world should fall around you, His arms will never let you go. He will protect, comfort and guide you all the days of your life. Choose to rest in Him. It's the only way to move beyond fatigue in your circumstances.

Calm your troubled heart with thoughts of His love and faithfulness, His goodness and Sovereignty. He will never leave or forsake you. He will work out all things for good, according to the perfect plan that He has for you. Those things that concern you concern Him and are under His absolute control at every moment. Nothing escapes His attention; nothing lies beyond what His eyes can see and His hands can control. Don't worry. All is well. When the winds blow and the waves toss your emotions and thoughts about, all is well. He is Lord of all things at all times. Rest in Him and find peace.[5]

---

5. Steve McVey, www.GraceWalk.com, "Overcoming Fatigue in Our Circumstances."

TRIALS AND PAIN

He knows the way that I take; when He has tested me, I shall come forth as gold. — Job[6]

Don't be weary in well doing: for in due season we shall reap, if we faint not. — Paul, the Apostle[7]

Father has said He will exalt you in due time, but remember, He is referring to His time and not yours!

Some of you are actually in a fiery furnace right now. You are in a special kind of spiritual testing. In Father's plan it may not yet be *"due time"* ... but it will come.[8]

Life is not over no matter how hard it may seem. It is Father's way that lies before you. Rest your weary heart in His immeasurable wisdom and unfailing sovereignty.

---

6. Job 23:10.
7. Galatians 6:9.
8. A.W. Tozer (1897-1963), *I Call It Heresy!* pages 116-117.

Chapter 7

"God Meant It For Good"

Even when apparently bad things happen in your life, it actually comes from the loving hands of your Father, Who knows what is genuinely best for your ultimate good, and that of everyone around us.

We can see this principle in the very first book of the Bible:

God meant it for good.[1]

These five words reveal that God's hand leaves no place in our lives untouched. Even that which seemingly is working against us is used by our Father to fulfill His Own good purpose in our lives.

These five words represent a powerful example demonstrated in the life of Joseph. His brothers had sold him into slavery. In what would appear to many as a very sad and unfortunate turn of events, Joseph eventually saw a divine appointment: "*God meant it for good.*"

---

1. Genesis 50:20.

But as for you, you thought evil against me; but God meant it for good, to bring to pass, as it is this day, to save much people alive.

Joseph *ultimately* would come to see that his *apparent* tragedy was God's plan to save his family (and Egypt as well, if not the whole world) from starvation during a famine. We should never be discouraged even in our severest trials. We can unreservedly trust God's steady, unfailing hand in *all* that we experience – in the *"good"* as well as in the apparent *"evil."* The knowledge that *"God meant it for good"* can settle the tired heart and bring peace to the worried mind.

Father has a plan, He's in control.

Rest in that.

Chapter 8

"I Create Evil"

God is the Creator and Controller of the apparent "evil," as well as He is of the good. Listen to this clear principle written by Isaiah, the Old Testament Prophet of Israel.

> *I form the light, and create darkness: I make peace, and* CREATE EVIL: *I the Lord do* ALL THESE THINGS.[1]

Many do not understand that God does *"all these things,"* including the creation of *"evil."* We must never forget that everything is about God. Nothing comes into our lives that is not from His hand – even things which looks to us as some great "evil." God has never lost control of *any* aspect of His universe – including ourselves. After all, what kind of "God" would He be if He could not control our lives? Including all the "bad" stuff that happens to us?

Though, initially, it is hard to grasp, God created *"evil"* as a part of His divine plan. It did not "sneak" into His creation; it wasn't brought in by some other means or creature. Rather,

---
1. Isaiah 45:7.

He put it there Himself – right in the *"middle"* of the Garden of Eden.² Everything, including the seeming "evil," is strategically designed for His *ultimate* glory and for the *eventual* and *lasting* good of *all* mankind!

Comprehension of these seven words – *"I the Lord do all these things"* – can change the way we look at *all things*, for, indeed, *all things are of God*.³ As with Joseph (*"God meant it for good"*), it is vital for us to understand that Father has His hands in everything that comes our way. He actively operates in and through *every* situation. As Frank Kujawa, writes,

> Whatever is said to us, or done to us, is actually being done by God. We can grow with this information. Others (actually God) come into our lives in order to purify us, to make us stronger. This means that whoever is bugging us the most, is exactly the one we need at the time, and we are to thank God for it ... So, we see God in all things ... And we cannot judge, because in essence we are judging God. And who are we to do that?

We must embrace the fact that our Father has a plan, and that He is in absolute control; after all,

He is God.

Rest in that.

---

2. Genesis 2:9.
3. II Corinthians 5:18.

Chapter 9

"Shall We Not Receive Evil?"

His wife said to him, "Do you still retain your integrity? Curse God, and die." But he said to her, "You speak as one of the foolish women speaks. What? Shall we receive good at the hand of God, and shall we not receive evil?" In all this did not Job sin with his lips.[1]

"Naked came I out of my mother's womb, and naked shall I return thither: the Lord gave, and the Lord has taken away; blessed be the name of the Lord." In all this Job sinned not, nor charged God foolishly.[2]

These words are from the life and experience of Job, from the Old Testament.

God *always* knows best. He never has an off day. Even "evil" plays a key part in our development and maturity. Job learned

---
1. Job 2:9-10.
2. Job 1:21-22.

to recognize that "good" as well as "evil" came from the very *"hand of God."* Many who profess to know God do not acknowledge this crucial truth. For them, even to suggest that "evil" comes to them from the *"hand of God"* is sinful; yet Job did just this – he declared it to be so with his own mouth, and God proclaimed of him,

> *In ALL THIS Job did not sin with his lips, nor charge God foolishly.*

God-given faith recognizes that the rain is as important as the sunshine, that the tears are as needed as laughter, and that the dark colors are as valuable in the tapestry as are the light. Like a building under construction, a painting yet wet and unfinished, a cake batter unbaked, a tapestry still being woven, a tree that has yet to reach maturity, we with patience await the Master's grand completion.

Job also learned that it is our Father, in His great wisdom, Who *"gives"* and *"takes away."* Through all of Job's trials he was able to *"bless the name of the Lord"* – even through the *"evil"* and the *"taking away."*

Paul, the Apostle, echoes this amazing spirit, when he writes,

> *In everything give thanks.*[3]

These are truly profound words, but even further than that, not only does he tell us to be thankful *"IN everything,"* but also *"FOR all things."*

> *Giving thanks always FOR all things to God and the Father in the name of our Lord Jesus Christ.*[4]

---

3. I Thessalonians 5:18.
4. Ephesians 5:20.

Chapter 10

"Though He Slay Me"

Though He slay me, yet will I trust in Him.
— Job[1]

After Job's many great trials, the only thing that Job really had left was his life, and even *it* seemed to be hanging only by a thread. Yet Job trusted God completely, even with his very life; and why wouldn't he? Job knew that everything he had was from the hand of God, even His life;

> *The Lord gave, and the Lord takes away; blessed be the name of the Lord.*[2]

God had given Job his life, just as He had breathed into Adam's *"nostrils the breath of life,"*[3] and he knew that this breath would *"return to God Who gave it"*[4] one day, just as it had to each of his ancestors.

Job unreservedly trusted God, even with his breath. After all, it was God's breath that filled his lungs. Even though he knew, sooner or later, that breath would depart and return

---
1. Job 13:15.
2. Job 1:21.
3. Genesis 2:7.
4. Ecclesiastes 12:7.

to God, he also knew that God loved him and would restore him from the power of the grave. Job had the firm expectation of resurrection!

> *For I know that my Redeemer lives, and that He shall stand at the latter day on the earth: and though after skin worms destroy this body, yet in my flesh shall I see God: Whom I shall see for myself, and my eyes shall behold, and not another; though my reins be consumed within me.*[5]

Job had trusted God in the face of every other enemy; and as with all of us, death would be his last enemy. Job even trusted God in this great enemy's face, because he knew that his Redeemer had the power over death.

Well did Paul write,

> *The last enemy that shall be destroyed is death.*[6]

With such confidence of faith, even as we experience life's greatest of trials,

> *The peace of God, that is superior to every frame of mind, shall be garrisoning your hearts and your apprehensions in Christ Jesus.*[7]

Rest in that.

---

5. Job 19:25-27.
6. I Corinthians 15:26.
7. Philippians 4:7.

Chapter 11

"But if Not"

Shadrach, Meshach and Abednego answered and said to the king, "O Nebuchadnezzar, we are not careful to answer you in this matter. If it be so, our God Whom we serve is able to deliver us from the burning fiery furnace, and He will deliver us out of your hand, O king. But if not, be it known to you, O king, that we will not serve your gods, nor worship the golden image which you have set up. —
Daniel, the prophet[1]

The "Three Hebrew Children," to put it lightly, were in a "tight spot." Their very lives were in the balance. The king held the power of their lives in his hands, or so he thought.

Shadrach, Meshach and Abednego knew that things are not always as they *appear* to be, and that what they saw with their eyes was not the real picture of the situation.

---

1. Daniel 3:16-18.

Despite the fact that King Nebuchadnezzar was an earthly monarch who *appeared* to have their destiny under his control, they knew that there was a heavenly Sovereign Who had all things under His control. They knew the truth, as we learn later in the book of Daniel, that,

> *The most High rules in the kingdom of men, and gives it to whomsoever He will.*[2]

> *All the inhabitants of the earth are reputed as nothing: and He does according to His will ... among the inhabitants of the earth: and none can stay His hand.*[3]

This is the great truth of God's sovereignty over the affairs of men taught throughout the Scriptures.

> *Are not You God in heaven? Do You not rule over all the kingdoms of the heathen? In Your hand is there not power and might, so that none are able to withstand You?*[4]

Likewise,

> *The king's heart is in the hand of the Lord, as the rivers of water: He turns it wherever He will.*[5]

In fact,

> *HE is a great King over all the earth.*[6]

It is these truths that gave the "Three Hebrew Children" their strength and courage. They knew that GOD WAS ABLE to deliver them! Listen again to their response.

---

2. Daniel 4:17, 25.
3. Daniel 4:35.
4. II Chronicles 20:6.
5. Proverbs 21:1.
6. Psalms 47:2.

> *Our God ... is **able** to deliver us from the burning fiery furnace ...*

It can bring great peace to any trial or situation that we face, to know in our hearts that *"Our God ... is **able** to deliver us."* Faith calls us to live daily in these words: *"Our God ... is able!"*

Yet faith is greater than all of this! Faith calls us to live beyond *"God ... is able!"* Listen to the rest of their response.

> *But if* [He does] *not* [deliver us], *be it known to you, O king, that we will not serve your gods, nor worship the golden image which you have set up.*

Here is the principle: *"But if not."* Just as with the "Three Hebrew Children," God is able to deliver us from all of our trials and troubles, however great they are; *but* if He does not, He is still our God, He is still in control, He still loves us, He still has our best interest at heart, and He is still working *"everything by the intention of His Own will!"*[7] Faith calls us to far greater heights, to live daily in these words: *"But if not!"*

We cannot always understand the great trials of life; from our vantage point we cannot always understand what is truly best for us and our loved ones; we cannot always clearly see the "big picture" for what it really is – from its eternal and heavenly perspective – but Father can!

Father is able to deliver you from your current situation that at this moment may seem so hopeless; *"but if not,"* nothing has changed: He is still OUR great God and Father, and sometimes in His great love and wisdom He has destined for you not deliverance, but endurance – and that by His unfailing grace.

---

7. Ephesians 1:11.

"God is able" to deliver us, and He may do just that – *"but if not"* – regardless of the situations that we face, our *Father is in absolute control.*

Rest in that.

Chapter 12

"Nevertheless"

Father, if You are willing, remove this cup from Me: NEVERTHELESS not My will, but Yours be done. — The Lord Jesus Christ[1]

We hardly ever know what is really best for us. What seems to us a great heartache and devastating loss, God may have determined, in His love and wisdom, to be to our advantage.

As our Lord Jesus Christ faced the agonizing prospects of Calvary, it caused Him tremendous trepidation. His entire being recoiled at the thoughts of what He was about to face and experience. It produced deep agony in His heart and soul.

> *And being in an AGONY He prayed more earnestly: and His sweat was as it were great drops of blood falling down to the ground.*[2]

---
1. Luke 22:42.
2. Luke 22:44.

His prayer to Father was for deliverance, that the cup of Calvary would pass from Him; but this would not be Father's will. Father had a grander plan that included a journey up Golgotha's shameful hill – and *Father always knows best.*

All of us who know the rest of the story are eternally thankful that God did not allow this cup to pass from our Lord. Indeed, this cup was at the center of Father's purpose for the ages. We are thankful that our Lord Jesus Christ did not attempt to resist Father's will, but rather learned obedience to His all-knowing, all-wise and all-loving destiny.

> *Though He were a Son, yet learned He* OBEDIENCE *by the things which He* SUFFERED.[3]

> *He* HUMBLED *Himself, and became* OBEDIENT *to death, even the death of the cross.*[4]

We, too, as sons of God, are being fashioned into the image of Christ, for this is our divine destiny;[5] and we, like Christ, must learn obedience through suffering. This is Father's path to glory, for Christ as well as us.

CHRIST'S PATH TO GLORY WAS THROUGH SUFFERING

> *Ought not Christ to have* SUFFERED *these things, and* [then] *to enter into His* GLORY?[6]

> *We see Jesus, Who was made a little lower than the angels for the* SUFFERING *of death, crowned with* GLORY

---

3. Hebrews 5:8.
4. Philippians 2:8.
5. Romans 8:29; I Corinthians 15:49; Philippians 3:21; I John 3:2.
6. Luke 24:26.

and honor; that He by the grace of God should taste death for every man.⁷

It became Him, for Whom are all things, and by Whom are all things, in bringing many sons to GLORY, to make the Captain of their salvation perfect through SUFFERINGS.⁸

[The prophets,] *searching what, or what manner of time the spirit of Christ which was in them did signify, when it testified beforehand the* SUFFERINGS *of Christ, and the* GLORY *that should follow.*⁹

OUR PATH TO GLORY IS
ALSO THROUGH SUFFERING

I calculate that the SUFFERINGS *of this present time are not worthy to be compared with the* GLORY *which shall be revealed in us.*¹⁰

Rejoice, seeing you are partakers of Christ's SUFFERINGS; *that, when His* GLORY *shall be revealed, you may be glad also with exceeding joy.*¹¹

The God of all grace, Who has called us to His GLORY, *lasting for the ages, by Christ Jesus, after that you have* SUFFERED *a while, make you perfect, establish, strengthen, settle you.*¹²

Like our Lord Jesus Christ, we may look at the situations and circumstances that are before us and pray that Father would

---

7. Hebrews 2:9.
8. Hebrews 2:10.
9. I Peter 1:11.
10. Romans 8:18.
11. I Peter 4:13.
12. I Peter 5:10.

let them pass. This is not a wrong request, since our Lord prayed it as well. Paul tells us,

> *Be anxious for nothing; but in everything by prayer and supplication with thanksgiving, let your requests be made known to God.*[13]

As per the instructions of Paul, and the example of Christ, we should pour our hearts out to our Father when they are heavy. We should tell Him what it is that we want, but we must also, with our Lord, submit our troubles and trials, as well as OURSELVES, to His wise and loving will: "NEVERTHELESS *not my will, but Yours be done.*"

Christ submitted Himself to the wise and loving will of His Father. We may look to Him, and see a pattern for our own times of trial.

> *Looking to Jesus the Author and Finisher of our faith; Who for the joy that was set before Him endured the cross, despising the shame, and is set down at the right hand of the throne of God.*[14]

Our Lord Jesus Christ endured the ordeal of Calvary, because a sequel had been set before Him – "*for the joy that was set before Him endured the cross.*"

Father's answer to us at times may be deliverance. More often than not, however, as in the case of our Savior, when we approach His GRACIOUS throne, what we find is His "*grace to help in time of need.*"

---

13. Philippians 4:6.
14. Hebrews 12:2.

> Let us therefore come boldly to the throne of grace, that we may obtain mercy, and find grace to help in time of need.[15]

When we pray for the cup of our own heavy burdens and trials to pass, may we also have the courage of faith to pray "NEVERTHELESS *not my will, but Yours be done.*" While deliverance may be in our hearts, may our hearts obediently submit to His wise and loving will; and with Christ we can – *for the joy set before us* – endure our trials.

The knowledge of FATHER's wise and loving will can settle the weary heart and bring peace to the troubled mind. Regardless of the situations that we face, *Father knows best.*

Rest in that.

---

15. Hebrews 4:16.

Chapter 13

YOU ARE HIS MASTERPIECE

For we are His workmanship. — Paul, the Apostle[1]

Sometimes life is filled with frustration, discouragement and guilt. These are all rooted in self-reliance, and are a failure to lay hold on the reality of God's workmanship in our lives.

We are *His* achievement![2] Think of it: God is busy achieving something in you. Regardless of how you see things or feel about it, God is at work in you!

> *Now to Him Who is able to do exceeding abundantly above all that we ask or think, according to the power that works in us.*[3]

> *For it is God Who works in you both to will and to do of His good pleasure.*[4]

---
1. Ephesians 2:10.
2. The *Concordant Version* renders the phrase in Ephesians 2:10 as, "*For His achievement are we.*"
3. Ephesians 3:20.
4. Philippians 2:13.

William R. Newell (1868-1956) well articulated the basis of the distresses of life:

> To "hope to be better" is to fail to see yourself in Christ only.
>
> To be disappointed with yourself, is to have believed in yourself.
>
> To be discouraged is unbelief – as to God's purpose and plan of blessing for you.

The fact is simple: we are not self-made; rather, we are God-made – *we are His workmanship, His achievement.* The great, wise and almighty God of the universe is steadily at work in your life. You are His handiwork.

Things are not as they appear. This divine work in our lives will culminate in "EVERY MAN" having the praise of God. This means that one day God will praise *you*. How could it be otherwise; for, after all, YOU ARE His workmanship!

> *Judge nothing before the time, until the Lord comes ... then shall **every man** have praise of God.*[5]

If it is true that God has made you and that you have not made yourself; if it is true that He began the work in you and will complete it, then why do you fret so? Why are you so anxious and troubled? Why are you so full of care, frustration and discouragement? After all, is He not God? Is He not in charge? Is not He the Creator, and you are His creature?

Regardless of the situations that we face, Father is in control – you are His workmanship – *you are His achievement.*

Rest in that.

---

5. I Corinthians 4:5.

Chapter 14

HE WILL FINISH WHAT HE STARTED

Being confident of this very thing, that He Who has begun a good work in you will perform it until the day of Jesus Christ. — Paul, the Apostle[1]

You are the handiwork of God. This is something about which Paul was *confident* – *"Being confident of* ***this very thing.***"

Father *"has begun a good work in you,"* and what He has started He will finish to completion. Paul did not have confidence in himself; rather his confidence was in Father.

Paul had written earlier,

> *To will is present with me; but how to* PERFORM *that which is good I find not.*[2]

Paul could not find how to *"perform"* that which was *"good."*

---

1. Philippians 1:6.
2. Romans 7:18.

Yet eventually he came to have confidence that Father would *"perform"* the *"good work"* that *He* had started in him. What we can never *"perform"* in and of ourselves, God Himself *"will perform."*

You are His work. He started you, and He *will* complete you. This is something about which you can be confident, because it is ALL of God. This is a divine process that He *Himself* will carry out to its completion. With Paul, we, too, can have the full *confidence* that He *"WILL perform it until the day of Jesus Christ!"*

Delighting in these great and glorious truths can settle the weary heart and bring peace to the troubled mind. Regardless of what appears to be happening in our lives, *Father is in control*, performing His work.

Rest in that.

Chapter 15

A Complaining Spirit

These are murmurers, complainers, walking after their own lusts. — Jude[1]

Do not be discontented. ... In all that you do, avoid grumbling. — The Apostle Paul[2]

Complaining is a prominent human pastime. We grumble and whine about the weather, our jobs, our spouses, our governments, our finances – just about our lives in general. Like spoiled children, discontentment is an unthankful heart-attitude of *protest* towards our heavenly Father. Our hearts gripe, huff, sulk, moan and bellyache about everything.

Ugh! Grrr!

---
1. Jude 1:16
2. I Corinthians 10:10, *Weymouth;* Philippians 2:14, *Moffatt*

Contentment: Complaining's Contrast

Contentment is a rare quality. It has been so from the beginning. Adam and Eve had abundant bounty from God's hand all around them. Only one thing was withheld from them: the Tree of the Knowledge of Good and Evil; but it was the very thing that they wanted and desired. This one thing kept them discontent: *if only* they could have the fruit from *this* tree their lives would be complete and fulfilled – or so they thought.

Discontentment is at the core of the human heart, whereas *contentment* is the Divine work – a heavenly learning process. The Apostle Paul tells us so. It was even necessary that he complete this course of spiritual instruction. Let's allow this variety of translations from Philippians 4:11 to speak truly to us.

> *I have learned, in whatsoever state I am, therewith to be content (KJV).*
>
> *As to me, I have learnt in those circumstances in which I am, to be satisfied ... (Darby).*
>
> *For my part I have learned, whatever be my outward experiences, to be content (Weymouth).*

Do you have spiritual ears to hear these words deep within your heart? Do they speak to you?

Paul goes on to write to Timothy of contentment's *"great gain."*

> *Godliness with contentment is great gain. For we brought nothing into this world, and it is certain we can carry nothing out. Having food and raiment let us be therewith content.*[3]

---
3. I Timothy 6:6-8.

The Antidote for Complaining Is Found in Thanksgiving

Thanksgiving is the divine answer to discontentment. Only faith from God can lay hold on the grand truth that *all things come from God*. This realization transforms human complaining into divine contentment!

All things are of God.[4]

For of Him, and through Him, and to Him, are ALL THINGS.[5]

There is but one God, the Father, of Whom are ALL THINGS.[6]

Here is the entrance of faith. The Scriptures make the plain, bold statement that *"all things are of God."* Therefore faith will have the daring audacity actually to thank Him for *"all things"* that come in life, and will, with Job, say,

Shall we receive good at the hand of God, and shall we not receive evil? The Lord gives, and the Lord takes away; blessed be the name of the Lord.[7]

All of Our Complaining Is Actually Against Father

When we complain about spouses, our governments, our jobs, our responsibilities, we are actually complaining against the SOURCE of *"all things."* It is crucial that we come to this realization: since everything comes from our heavenly Father, our discontentment and complaining, our grumbling

---
4. II Corinthians 5:18.
5. Romans 11:36.
6. I Corinthians 8:6.
7. Job 2:10; 1:22.

and whining, is all directly against Him. It is a lack or lapse of faith in Him – in His sovereign, loving control of His Own universe.

When we bewail our wife or husband, rail against and mock our president, lament and criticize our employer, bemoan the downward turn of our financial circumstances, these are all actually directed to God. When Adam ate the forbidden fruit of Eden's garden his complaint and accusation against God was, that it was *"the woman whom You gave to me ..."*[8]

Oh, that Father would grant us the faith to hear this same complaint and accusation in ourselves!

THANKING FATHER FOR *EVERYTHING*

Here is the greatest lesson of life, what life is all about: Truly trusting Father *in everything,* to the point that we also are thanking Him *for everything* – *"bad"* things as well as *"good"* the *"taking away"* as well as the *"giving."*

Faith is the God-given spiritual courage and strength actually to believe Him *regardless of the circumstances* – that daring unmatched boldness simply to believe Him over our emotions, over our senses, over our desires, that plain audacity of faith just to believe Him!

We will explore this more in the next chapter.

---

8. Genesis 3:12.

Chapter 16

GIVING FATHER THANKS FOR ALL THINGS

In everything give thanks: for this is the will of God in Christ Jesus concerning you. ... Giving thanks always for all things to God and the Father in the name of our Lord Jesus Christ. — Paul, the Apostle[1]

These powerful words of Paul are worthy of capturing our attention.

First, he tells us to be thankful *"IN everything"* – regardless of the circumstances; then, to be thankful *"FOR all things."*

Notice to whom Paul instructs that thanks is to be given: *"to God"* for *"all things."*

If your mother gave you a gift of an apple pie she had made, would you send a "thank you" for it to your mechanic? Of course not! That simply would be ridiculous. Certainly, you would thank your mother who gave it to you. The only reason

---
1. I Thessalonians 5:18; Ephesians 5:20.

we would thank God **FOR** *"all things"* is that *"***ALL THINGS***"* actually came from God. All things – *every last one of them!* Listen to how clearly the Apostle Paul makes this truth known:

> ***All things*** *are of God.*[2]
>
> *For of Him, and through Him, and to Him, are **all things**.*[3]
>
> *There is but one God, the Father, of Whom are **all things**.*[4]

Here lies the entrance of faith. The Scriptures make the plain, bold statement that *"all things are of God."* Therefore, faith will have the audacity actually to thank Him for *"all things"* that come in life, and will with Job of the Old Testament say,

> *Shall we receive good at the hand of God, and shall we not receive evil? The Lord gives, and the Lord takes away; blessed be the name of the Lord.*[5]

Here is the greatest lesson of life – what life is all about: Truly trusting our heavenly Father *in* everything, to the point that we also are thanking Him *for* everything.

Faith is the divinely given courage to believe Father regardless of the circumstances – that daring spiritual boldness simply to believe Him over our emotions, over our senses, over our creeds, over what others might say – that plain audacity just to believe the actual words of God!

Thank God *for **everything!***

---

2. II Corinthians 5:18.
3. Romans 11:36.
4. I Corinthians 8:6.
5. Job 2:10; 1:22.

Chapter 17

REAL LIFE

Do not squander time, for that is the stuff life is made of. — Benjamin Franklin

Real life takes place *every* day, in *every* circumstance. Sometimes we can get caught up in the postponing of living. We end up wishing our lives away, thinking that we will *really start living* come Friday, come payday, when we start our new job, when we get married, when our kids are grown, when we retire, etc.

Life is such a wonderful gift, directly from the hand of God. Each day is a precious expression of His sheer goodness to us. We honor Him by living out this gift to its fullest.

Granted, life is filled with troubles; yet as we handle their details, let's not fret, but rejoice that we are alive to do so, for life is filled abundantly with more than just trouble. Stand in wonder and amazement at the fresh handiwork of God that is all around us. It is there for the watchful eye.

> *The Lord's mercies ... are **new every morning**.*[1]

> *The goodness of God **continually** endures.*[2]

Live in the day! Enjoy life in each of its moments. Don't live in the past, or in the future. Today is God's gift to you – the present.

Many days from our past may call for us to live in them – with their failures and regrets. "What if I had made a different choice?" "What if I hadn't moved?" "What if I had taken that job?" "What if …?" By giving ourselves over to these "What ifs," we waste and lose our precious life now – the present.

Then there are our imagined days of the future – how they beckon to us to give them our attention, with all of their fears and anxieties regarding the unknown. "What if I lose my health?" "What if the stock market falls?" "What if my spouse dies?" "What if …?" Don't lose the present on your runaway train of imagined scenarios about the future. These endless "possibilities" that your mind can conjure will only rob you of the real life that God has given you today.

> *Therefore don't worry about tomorrow: for tomorrow will take care of itself. Enough for each day are its own troubles.*[3]

Let's not allow our "What if …" imaginations of our past or future to lay claim to our present from God. Allow God to transform our mind, casting down our *"imaginations."*

> *Casting down imaginations, and every high thing that exalts itself against the knowledge of God, and bringing*

---
1. Lamentations 3:22-23
2. Psalm 52:1
3. Matthew 6:34.

Real Life

into captivity every thought to the obedience of Christ.[4]

How can we not praise and magnify our good and gracious Creator *every* new day? How can we not do so from hearts filled with the joy of His life? How can we who know Him be genuinely tempted to murmur and complain, to fret and fuss? We are alive! – and not just alive, but alive with *His very life!*

For in Him we live, and move, and have our being.[5]

Live. Live every day. Live in the moment.

---

4. II Corinthians 10:5.
5. Acts 17:28.

Chapter 18

REAL WORSHIP

Worship God in the spirit. – Paul, the Apostle[1]

Life is to be worship. All of it – every day, in every place, in every circumstance – is where real worship is to take place. It's not reserved for certain times, at specific places or special circumstances.

God can be worshiped easily for His supply of food, clothing, housing and other provisions, although few rarely do even that. He most certainly can be worshiped for His rich provision of redemption, salvation, justification, even though not many do so regularly. However, the greatest height of worship is not to be found in any of these.

The true summit of worship is not in the context of the "good" things that come into our lives, but in the apparently "evil" ones. It is one thing to worship God when things are going "our way." It is quite another issue to worship Him genuinely when things are not going well at all, when the circumstances seem as though they are "evil" – even desperately so.

---
1. Philippians 3:3

To bow our hearts in humble, sincere, submissive worship before Him, even when all of our being – our senses, our desires, our passions, our understanding and our hearts – cringe and recoil from our current lot: this is the pinnacle of true worship.

We see this clearly in the Scripture's account of Job. All at once the circumstances of His life turned horribly wrong. His health, wealth and children were all gone. His weary mind, body and heart – every core part of him – must have demanded a compelling, "No!" Every fiber of his being must have been in active protest. However, something far greater than all of this was in Job's heart as well: faith in the faithful, Sovereign Creator. He knew that God was God in all of the wonderful things in his life, as well as in all of his calamity. He knew that ultimately all was from God's hand, the "good" as well as the apparent "evil."

> *Shall we receive good at the hand of God, and shall we not receive evil?*[2]

> *The Lord gave, and the Lord has taken away; blessed be the name of the Lord.*[3]

Now *there* is the greatest height of worship: worshipping God in everything – the *"good"* as well as the *"evil,"* the *"giving"* as well as the *"taking away."* The worship of God every day, in every place, in every circumstance – this is true worship. When in the face of *"evil"* and *"taking away"* we learn with Job to *"bless the name of the Lord,"* then we, too, will come to know the true meaning of real worship.

> *I will bless the Lord **at all times**: His praise shall continually be in my mouth.*[4]

---

2. Job 2:10
3. Job 1:21-22
4. Psalm 34:1

Chapter 19

Mornings and Evenings

Vanity of vanities; all is vanity ... I have seen all the works that are done under the sun; and, behold, all is vanity. — King Solomon[1]

King Solomon describes for us the futility of life apart from the Creator. It is simply vain and empty when viewed apart from the Sovereign, loving God Who is your Father. It is extremely hard to go through life apart from the knowledge that He is in complete control.

King David reminds us that,

> *The steps of a man are ordered by the Lord.*[2]

He also wrote that our days,

> *All of them were written in Your book; the days, they were formed when there was not one of them.*[3]

---
1. Ecclesiastes 1:2, 14.
2. Psalm 37:23.
3. Psalm 139:16.

Think of this wonderful truth. All of your days were written down by God, designed before any of them ever had been lived. Many live their daily lives without recognition of this stabilizing truth of the One Who *"works everything by the intention of His Own will."*[4] They approach their days, and struggle through them, as the masters of their own lives.

For those who live as though they were in charge of their lives, two of the hardest parts of the day are waking up in the morning and going to bed in the evening.

In the mornings, days are greeted with uncertainty as thoughts of the "What if ..." trials and challenges of the day press in on the mind and heart. There is a waking up to varying degrees of uneasiness, concern, apprehension, worry and anxiety; even at times to overwhelming fear, dread and depression. Feelings of inadequacy and uncertainty press in.

In the evenings, days are retired with the annoying "What if ..." reflections of its happenings. There is second guessing, regret and disappointment. Feelings of frustration, dissatisfaction and failure settle in; even at times shame, guilt and worthlessness.

After all, they see themselves as the lords of their own lives, the captains of their own ships and the masters of their own destiny. With this view comes the recurring cycle of vanity of which King Solomon spoke.

> *Vanity of vanities; all is vanity ... What profit has a man of all his labor which he takes under the sun? One generation passes away, and another generation comes: but the earth abides. The sun also arises, and the sun goes down, and hastens to his place where he arose ... All*

---

4. Ephesians 1:11.

things are full of labor; man cannot express it: the eye is not satisfied with seeing, nor the ear filled with hearing.[5]

Why is man's life filled with such vanity; such futility, emptiness, barrenness, purposelessness and aimless frustration? Because he has been subjected so by his Creator.

For the creature was made subject to vanity, not willingly, but by reason of Him Who has subjected the same in hope.[6]

"*Vanity*" is the lot of earthly man. Yet for one who trusts their Heavenly Father, quite another view prevails! Instead of being bound to such emptiness, they can rise to heights of divine life.

Solomon's perspective showed the vanity of the human viewpoint without God. Paul, the apostle, has given us a perspective "*far above all heavens,*" revealing the true purpose found only in the divine viewpoint: "*your labor is* NOT IN VAIN *in the Lord.*"[7]

Those of us who know Father as the great Planner and Director of our days have a completely different approach to our mornings and evenings – and the entire unfolding of every minute of our day.

In the mornings, days can be greeted with the joy and excitement of knowing that *they,* as well as ourselves, are His. The uncertainties of the "What if ..." viewpoint are divinely transformed into the eager anticipation of seeing what God has planned for the day. We are able to awaken to the thrill of knowing that we will be witnesses of the unfolding of His detailed plan and purpose for our day. His presence presses

5. Ecclesiastes 1:2-8.
6. Romans 8:20.
7. I Corinthians 15:58.

in on our minds. There is a waking up to peace and joy as we know that our life, with all of its daily circumstances, is firmly in His hand, and carried out by His capable direction. Our hearts are able to say, "Today we are on the great adventure of faith!"

In the evenings, when the day is over, we can rest our heads on our pillows and with surety and confidence regarding our day say, "This was the will of God." The "What if ..." reflections of its happenings are transformed into a place of peace and rest – knowing that the will of God was done, and who could have prevented it? The realization of our divine appointment is able to settle within our hearts and minds. After all, *He* is the Lord of our life, the Captain of our ship, the Master of our destiny. Daniel the prophet wrote that,

> *God does according to His will in the army of heaven, and among the inhabitants of the earth: and none can prevent His hand.*[8]

You have the joy of waking up each morning as His *clay*.

You have the anticipation of living each day as His *handiwork*.

You have the rest of laying your heads on your pillows each night as His *achievement*.

---

8. Daniel 4:35.

About Others

Chapter 20

SEEING OTHERS AS FATHER DOES

I see men as trees, walking. — former blind man[1]

In Mark's Gospel we read an interesting encounter that our Lord Jesus Christ had with a blind man. Jesus healed him, but Jesus's first touch only partially restored his sight – he could only see men as walking tress. That is, his sight was such that the only way he could distinguish between men and trees was by the fact that the men were moving about, or walking. After a *second* touch of the Savior's hand, then his sight was completely restored and he *"saw every man clearly."*[2]

Set in its Jewish context, the account obviously has a direct application to Israel as a nation. It will require a second divine touch for them to see clearly.[3] This is true not only of God's

---

1. Mark 8:24.
2. Mark 8:22-25.
3. A.E. Knoch shows us the application of this miracle to the nation of Israel:

dealing with Israel, but it is often His method of dealing with us as well. Paul the Apostle prays for those who *already* know God, that the eyes of their understanding might be further enlightened.[4] This has been the experience of many. Not until God has done a *greater* work in their hearts can their eyes fully be opened so that they can see *"every man clearly"* for who they really are: loved of Father.

The far-reaching, triumphant work of our Lord Jesus Christ on Calvary was not limited to certain individuals. He was not partial in His work and accomplishments – He was all-inclusive. Christ did His wonderful work not just for a few, but for *all*.[5]

Paul discloses this magnificent truth of reconciliation to God.

*God was in Christ, **reconciling the world to Himself**.*[6]

*Having made peace through the blood of His cross, by Him **to reconcile all things to Himself;** by Him, I say, whether they are things in earth, or things in heaven.*[7]

> The Lord could have healed him completely in an instant, but He did not choose to do so. It is evidently another sign, and we will find its meaning in the restoration of Israel's spiritual sight ... At first the blind man's sight was blurred. Later he saw clearly. So it was with Israel. In the past they saw that there would be a gradual growth, like a tree, until the kingdom. But it will take another application of His hands in the future to restore them. Then they will no longer be puzzled by the course of events. Throughout the past proclamation of the kingdom, especially in the Pentecostal era, the prospect of the kingdom was vague. It will not be so at the time of the end. — *Concordant Commentary on the New Testament* (1968), page 71

4. Ephesians 1:18.
5. For further information on this issue, see the excellent resources at: www.SalvationofAll.com
6. II Corinthians 5:19.
7. Colossians 1:20.

We, too, now can see *"every man clearly"* in their relationship to the all-inclusive Father of reconciliation. The more we learn of Him, the more we will see things and people as He sees them.

Chapter 21

Trusting Others to Father

I entrust you to God. — Paul, the Apostle[1]

Do you carry the heavy weight of others on your shoulder, feeling that somehow you are responsible for the direction and outcome of their lives?

Being "God" to someone is an especially hard job if you are not qualified. There is only One in the universe qualified for such a daunting task, and He already has all things squarely under His control. So, relax.

God is good at His job. Just like with any other work, you can't judge the finished product when seeing it in some stage of its development. This is true of you and me, of our loved ones and friends – all of God's creation!

When a dinner is being prepared the kitchen may look like a big mess, and the ingredients in their various stages of being mixed, stirred, blended, pounded, chopped, heated, etc. may not taste good or seem as if they will ever amount to anything. It is all just a matter of timing in the kitchen of the master chef. Just wait until the finished product is taken

---
1. Acts 20:32 (*Moffatt*).

from the kitchen of preparation and placed on the table of display!

So it is with all of God's creation. He is still mixing the batter – with all of us. After all, it was to the idol worshipping pagans that Paul said,

> For in Him WE live, and move, and have our being.[2]

Don't be depressed as you look around you. What you see is NOT the end of God's plan and purpose. What you see is NOT the finished product of God. God is actively at work in us, in every circumstance of every life.

God Who works *"everything by the intention of His Own will"* finds no challenge with the circumstances and lives of our loved ones – not even the hard cases. Nothing poses an obstacle to Him – after all, He *is* the Almighty God.

God may have chosen you to be one of His instruments of ministry toward your loved ones; but never forget that you are the instrument and not the craftsman. Just as the spoon, the sifter and the whisk are all just tools in the hands of the cook, so it is with you. You are but the utensil in the hands of the Master Chef. Just as these instruments have no life and purpose of their own to create any dish, but must be selected and used by the cook at his own will, so it is with you.

Do not be overwhelmed or discouraged: you are NOT the Workman, but only the utensil in His hand. Whatever comes out of His use of you is completely up to Him.

Relax with those whom God has placed in your life. God is God; He is in charge. He loves them just as unconditionally

---

2. Acts 17:28.

Trusting Others to Father

as He loves you. He is molding them, as surely as he is you – day-by-day – into *all* that He intends for them to be, regardless of what we may think we currently see.

Do not be tempted to play "God" in the lives of others. Do not be disheartened with His pace, nor with His progress, for He is not yet finished; *but one day,* you and I and all of our loved ones finally will be complete. Trust others to Father.

Chapter 22

GIVE YOURSELF AND OTHERS SOME SLACK

With all humility and meekness, with patience, bearing with each other in love. —
Paul, the Apostle[1]

We all are very broken people, marred in the Potter's hands. We all are very busy people, attending to the many details of life. We all are very composite people, coming from so many different backgrounds, and journeying down such diverse roads, with varied influences. Patience is so essential in our relationships with each other.

God's work in your life is a slow, gradual process. All growth is progressive, and the finer the organism, the longer the process. An oak tree takes a hundred years to mature, yet on the other hand a squash takes only two to three months, depending on the variety.

Miles Stanford reminds us that,

> The temptation to shortcut is especially strong unless we see the value of and submit to the necessity of the time element, in simple trust resting in His hands,

---
1. Ephesians 4:2.

"being confident of this very thing, that He which began a good work in you will perform it until the day of Jesus Christ" (Philippians 1:6).

Dear friends, it will take a long time! – but since God is working [for the ages], why should we be concerned about the time involved?

You are God's oak tree. He has dedicated Himself to His work in you for the long haul. So, cut yourself and others some slack.[2]

---

2. *The Principles of Spiritual Growth,* chapter 2.

Chapter 23

Don't Let Them Agitate You!

Take a Deep Breath and Relax in Father

> *Peace I leave with you, My peace I give to you: not as the world gives, give I to you. Let not your heart be troubled, neither let it be afraid.* – The Lord Jesus Christ[1]

> *The peace of God, which passes all understanding, shall keep your hearts and minds through Christ Jesus. ... Let the peace of God rule in your hearts.* – Paul, the Apostle[2]

There surely is much uncertainty and turmoil in the world around us; but there is one thing that we need to remember: God is not *ruffled* by earthly events and de-

---
1. John 14:27.
2. Philippians 4:7; Colossians 3:15.

tails. This is because He *is* GOD, and He *is* in sovereign control of *everything*. Simply put, this means that God is at peace – no wringing of His hands, no wiping of sweat from His brow – after all, Paul calls Him the *"God of peace."*³

You have *"peace with God"* because of the work of our Lord Jesus Christ on Calvary. *All* enmity and strife between you and God has been permanently removed. We, who once were estranged from God in our hearts and minds, can enjoy *"peace with God through our Lord Jesus Christ."*⁴

Not only has Christ provided you *"peace **with** God,"* but you can also enjoy *"the peace **of** God."* In fact, your heavenly Father desires that you rest *with Him* in every detail of life, enjoying His very Own unworried and tranquil spirit. You can *let the **peace of God** rule in your heart*.⁵ In other words, He desires to take charge of all of your cares, concerns and worries; the peace of His Own nature and character *settling*⁶ your heart!

The *peace of God* can be yours through a simple trust. So, *don't let anyone or anything agitate you*. Rest in your heavenly Father. He loves you and always knows best.

Who or what manages to get under your skin and causes you to lose your peace? Are they *bigger* than He? Do they in any way threaten Father, or His plan for you? Can they derail His purpose for you? Certainly not! If He is the God of the universe, then why allow yourself to be agitated by your circumstances, or by others?

Listen to Paul's wonderful words of encouragement to us,

---

3. Romans 15:33; 16:20; Philippians 4:9; I Thessalonians 5:23.
4. Romans 4:25; 5:1.
5. Colossians 3:15.
6. "Settle" is the word used in the Weymouth translation of Colossians 3:15.

> *Be anxious for nothing;* but in everything by prayer and supplication with thanksgiving let your requests be made known to God. And the peace of God, which passes all understanding, shall keep your hearts and minds through Christ Jesus.[7]

God is *never* caught surprised. He knows *exactly* what He is doing. You can have complete confidence in Him, because nothing is outside of His sovereign control. Therefore, you need not be overwhelmed and defeated by the adversities of life.

Life is empty when viewed apart from the sovereign, loving God Who is your Father. After all, if we see ourselves as the lords of our own lives, the captains of our own ships and the masters of our own destiny, we will experience only the recurring cycle of emptiness; as all areas of life illustrate and demonstrate the barrenness of life apart from God.[8]

Those who know Father as the great Planner and Director of our days can know His Own peace in our lives. This *peace of God* that can be ours has nothing to do with family, neighborhood, civil, social or national peace. This is about *our hearts* aligned with God *and* His purpose, which alone brings quietness and peace to our hearts and lives.

No matter in what circumstances you may find yourself, you can remain calm, peaceful and happy, knowing that your heavenly Father is in *absolute* control. Ultimately, your disposition towards the circumstances of your life reflects your disposition toward God Himself. Aligning your disposition with His will bring a change of quietness and peace to your life.

---

7. Philippians 4:6.
8. Ecclesiastes 1:2-8.

Many live in needless turmoil created by the misjudging of the true source of *all things*.[9] Don't allow others to agitate you. Don't allow your circumstances to disturb your enjoyment of the life that your heavenly Father has given to you.

Take a deep breath and relax in Him.

---

9. *All things are of God* (II Corinthians 5:18).

About God

Chapter 24

ALL OF YOUR DAYS WERE WRITTEN IN HIS BOOK

My days, all of them were written in Your book; the days, they were formed when there was not one of them. – King David[1]

Find comfort in knowing that God knew you long before you were ever born. It is reassuring to understand that the details of your life today were written in His book before you ever lived them. It should be a cause of rest to your heart to know that He has designed the details of your life; that you're not living your life on your own, but that He is God – large and in charge – of all that today, and every other day, brings forth.

After all, He is the God Who declares,

> The end from the beginning ... and ... from ancient times the things that are not yet done.[2]

---

1. Psalm 139:16.
2. Isaiah 46:9-10.

It is a great relief to recognize that you can neither disappoint Him nor surprise Him as you live out your day; for He alone is the Author of your life, the Sovereign Scribe Who has masterfully crafted the script of your days on the pages of His epic work.

You are not self-made: you are *God-made*. You are *"His workmanship," "His achievement"*[3] and, of course,

> *Known to God are all His works from the beginning of the ages.*[4]

You can rejoice today that you are His, and that He is fully in charge of your days.

> *For in Him we live, and move, and have our being.*[5]

Little wonder that King David wrote:

> *I will praise You; for I am fearfully and wonderfully made: marvelous are Your works; and that my soul knows right well. My frame was not hidden from You, when I was made in secret, and skillfully wrought in the lowest parts of the earth. My days, all of them were written in Your book; the days, they were formed when there was not one of them. How precious also are Your thoughts to me, O God! How great is the sum of them! If I should count them, they are more in number than the sand: when I awake, I am still with You.*[6]

---

3. Ephesians 2:10.
4. Acts 15:18.
5. Acts 17:28.
6. Psalm 139:14-18.

Chapter 25

STAGES OF LIFE

To everything there is a season, and a time to every purpose under the heaven: a time to be born, and a time to die; a time to plant, and a time to pluck up that which is planted; a time to kill, and a time to heal; a time to break down, and a time to build up. — King Solomon[1]

Every form of life that God has created has noticeable and predictable stages of growth. Awareness of these stages allows for a better understanding and a fuller appreciation of life.

Interestingly, there are a number of similar patterns in all forms of life. Early stages of growth often can be characterized by tremendous energy and acceleration of growth. Then there are periodic plateaus that take place along the way. This is the lesson of nature. We see these lulls clearly demonstrated with regularity:

---

1. Ecclesiastes 3:1-3.

- There is the night of the day –
  The daily recurring cycle of night

- There is the night of the month –
  The monthly recurring cycle of the moon

- There is the night of the year –
  The yearly recurring cycle of winter

Our own personal growth and development occurs neither at the rate, nor by the methods that we sometimes imagine. Instead, God works steadily and effectually for His Own purpose. He is in no rush, as if He was on some mere human schedule. Though His divine work may not be done in accordance with our own timetables, or by our predetermined methods or standards, He is nevertheless busy with His sure plan in our lives.

We should not be discouraged at the progress of our Father's work in our development, or of the seemingly unproductive plateaus. He is the Creator, we are His creatures. He is the Potter, we are His clay. He is the Workman, and we are His workmanship.

To **EVERYTHING** *there is a season.*

Chapter 26

The Long Process of Growth

Him Who works everything by the intention of His Own will. — Paul, the Apostle[1]

The Master Potter is faithfully and steadily at work in you. Make no mistake about it: He works *all things* after His Own will.

His hand in your life leaves *no* place untouched. Even that which seemingly is working against you is used by your Father to fulfill His Own good purpose in your life.[2]

This truth can be seen in the powerful example demonstrated in the life of Joseph, from the Old Testament. His brothers had sold him into slavery. This had been, on the surface, a very sad and unfortunate turn of events; but Joseph eventually was able to see in it all a divine purpose:

> *As for you, you thought evil against me; but God meant it for good.*[3]

---
1. Ephesians 1:11.
2. Romans 8:28.
3. Genesis 50:20.

At times God may even lead you through *"the valley of the shadow of death;"* but as long as you realize that He is with you, even the darkest, lowest valley can really be your *high ground!*

> *Yea, though I walk through the valley of the shadow of death, I will fear no evil: for You are with me; Your rod and Your staff, they comfort me.* — King David[4]

Paul, the Apostle, experienced such gut-wrenching hardness that, at times, he even *"despaired of life,"*

> *We were pressed out of measure, above strength, insomuch that we despaired even of life.*[5]

However, he was quick to add,

> *But we had the sentence of death in ourselves, that we should not trust in ourselves, but in God Who raises the dead.*[6]

The fact is quite simple: *you can trust God.* He alone is truly trustworthy; and He has a definite goal in sight for you! Your Father is taking you on a journey that will find its full completion in resurrection.

To take you on this journey will mean many years of wilderness and valleys. His goal is to bring you to a place where you find your completeness, satisfaction, contentment, glory, thanksgiving and rejoicing in Him alone, and not in your circumstances. This is what faith is all about: *not* in focusing on the circumstances all around you, but focusing on Father Who loves you unconditionally, unreservedly, undiminishingly, unendingly and unfailingly.

---

4. Psalm 23:4.
5. II Corinthians 1:8.
6. II Corinthians 1:9.

The Long Process of Growth

God is Love.[7]

Love never fails.[8]

God loves you greatly.[9]

Nothing can separate you from His love.[10]

You can love Him because He first loved you.[11]

---

7. I John 4:8, 16.
8. I Corinthians 13:8.
9. Ephesians 2:4.
10. Romans 8:35-37.
11. I John 4:19.

Chapter 27

JUST HOW MUCH GOD IS YOUR GOD?

The answer to this question will *greatly* affect your daily life. That God *is* God seems so basic enough that it goes without saying; but over and over in Scripture God reasserts His Godhood. The reason? There are those who would teach of a "god" who is somehow something less than "God."

Just how much "God" is God?

He is **ALL** GOD! In the Scriptures He repeatedly declares: *I am God.*[1]

We can learn a lot about God from His name. The basic Hebrew word used for God is *El*. The word means "Placer, Subjector." God is the *El* of Scripture. He is the Supreme Placer, the Supreme Subjector.

---

1. Genesis 35:11; 46:3; Psalm 46:10; 50:7; Isaiah 43:12; 45:22; 46:9; Ezekiel 28:9; Hosea 11:9.

Scriptures teach us that *EL* is able to do all;[2] He knows all;[3] He is present everywhere at the same time;[4] and He is the producer of all.[5]

He is the Creator, the Owner and the Proprietor. He is Planner and Executor. He is Supplier and Sustainer. He wills all, He orders all, He directs all. He is **GOD!**

Sadly, there are some who would teach of "a god" who somehow is less than THE GOD – that "he" can't seem to manage to do exactly what "he" wants to do, and that "he" is somehow actually subject to "his" own creatures. This may be "a god" of religion, but it is not THE GOD of Scripture.

Purely and simply, regardless of what His creatures may assert to the contrary – even by those who profess to represent Him, *the true and living God of Scripture is 100% absolute God and the Sovereign of His Own universe.*

Regardless of what man says about God to the contrary, God *is* GOD! Period.

Rest in that.

---

2. Omnipotent.
3. Omniscient.
4. Omnipresent.
5. Omniparous.

Chapter 28

THE CONTRASTS OF LIFE

In the beginning God created the heaven and the earth. — Moses[1]

Life is all about contrasts. They are everywhere and in everything. This is how we learn.

The very first verse of the Bible introduces us to *divinely appointed contrasts*. In the beginning God created two contrasting spheres: *the heaven, and the earth.* This is a key contrast that continues throughout the entire Scripture. When God makes things that are different, they are not the same.

In fact, *divinely appointed contrasts* are at the heart of understanding life. They are God's education tools, and He literally has filled our lives with these critical contrasts. If we can learn this, we will understand one of the most important principles of life:

---

1. Genesis 1:1

God / Man	Poverty / Wealth	Truth / Error
Male / Female	Feast / Famine	Hard / Soft
Heaven / Earth	Drought / Flood	Strength / Weakness
Divine / Human	Rough / Smooth	
Adult / Child	Good / Evil	Honor / Dishonor
Day / Night	Sweet / Bitter	Large / Small
Black / White	Sharp / Dull	Front / Back
Sunshine / Rain	Snow / Rain	Up / Down
Hot / Cold	Joy / Sorrow	Wet / Dry
Hungry / Full	Happy / Sad	War / Peace
Summer / Winter	Victory / Defeat	Bondage / Liberty
Spring / Autumn	Comfort / Pain	Life / Death
Sickness / Health	Love / Hate	

These are all carefully designed contrasts from God's hand – and make no mistake about it: these contrasts are *all* His creation. They are His firmly established method of teaching us.

God uses contrasts to bring us to divine knowledge and to a true appreciation of Who He really is, so that we may with joy and thanksgiving appreciate all that flows from His benevolent nature. In this principle of contrasts we ultimately will find the answers to all of our questions of life.

If we can realize this principle, we can learn to take a deep breath and relax.

A.E. Knoch (1874-1965), in his classic work, *The Problem of Evil*, helps us understand the divine necessity for such contrasts:

> Before they sinned, Adam and Eve had no knowledge of good. Good lay all about them, unmixed with evil. Health, strength, honor and companionship with one another and with God was their constant possession and privilege. Yet they knew nothing of the blessedness of these benefits. This we learn from the name given to the tree

which bore the forbidden fruit. To many minds it suggests only the knowledge of evil, rather than good. Yet, first and foremost, it was the tree of the knowledge of good.

Thus at the very forefront of revelation we have the principle suggested which is the key to unlock the great problems that most perplex us. It is this: *All knowledge is relative: it is based on contrast.* The knowledge of good is dependent upon the knowledge of evil. Hence the tree in the garden was not, as we usually think of it, merely the means of knowing evil, it was the means, primarily, of the knowledge of *good*. Adam and Eve had good, but did not realize it because they had had no experience of evil.

The perfection of Eden's garden was greatly lacking in the one element most dear to God's heart: Adam did not and could not apprehend God's goodness. There is not the slightest hint of Adam's appreciation or thanks, or worship or adoration. He received all as a matter of course and was quite incapable of discerning or responding even to that measure of divine love which lies on the surface of His goodness. If *we* should suddenly be transformed into glorious sinless beings and transported to such scenes of sylvan perfection, we would exult and praise the Author of our bliss. Not so with Adam. He knew no joy, for he knew no misery. He knew no good, for he knew no evil.

This point is most important, and we press it because it seems to be universally ignored and misrepresented. The garden of Eden has become a symbol of perfect bliss; we are always being reminded of its delights, and the happiness of the first pair has passed into a proverb. Yet there is not the slightest reason to suppose that Adam was delighted, or enjoyed the bliss ascribed to him. The mere possession of good does not give a knowledge or realization of it. Adam had perfect health, but what was that to one who never had even heard of disease? He had abundant food, but that was nothing to him who had never felt a famine. Even pleasure had no appeal to one who had known no pain.

The fatal lack in all of the perfection of Eden was the utter absence of any note of praise or thankfulness. Knowing no good, and utterly unacquainted with mercy or grace, Adam's heart was utterly incapable of love or adoration or worship. God's goodness did not receive the least response, because it was unknown. All that He had bestowed on Adam failed to kindle the affection for which He longed, and which is the goal of all of His gifts.

How could this grave defect be remedied? There was but one way, and that way was, in the wisdom of God, provided by the tree which He placed in the midst of the garden. Had Adam and Eve known good they would have treasured God's goodness and never would have forfeited it by disobeying His command. Yet, when they did eat of the tree, they set in motion the very forces which would remedy the defect which caused them to do it. What divine wisdom do we see here displayed! God's blessings being unappreciated, they offend Him by their deed and in so doing pave the way for an appreciation which satisfies both. Love is a marvelous schemer!

Had Adam never sinned he would have been a neutral, a sentient clod unfit for the full companionship of his Creator. Of one thing we may be sure: He would never have known evil; and we may be equally sure that he never would have known good. He would not curse God for sin, neither would he thank Him for His beneficence nor adore Him for His grace. He would have utterly failed to fulfill the purpose of His creation. We must always remember that the tree of the knowledge of good and evil had a double function. No one forgets that it brought the knowledge of *evil*; but it was primarily the tree of the knowledge of *good*. Adam had no appreciation of the good by which he was surrounded. Having known nothing else, it was not good to him. He received it as a matter of course, without a thankful thought.

Adam could have lived on indefinitely in such an unappreciated paradise, but only with untold loss to himself and to his Creator. All that he saw was God's hand; His heart was veiled. Some means must be found to rouse Adam's affectionate response to the Divine yearnings. He must learn to appreciate good. How shall this be done?

It is a notable fact, and full of significance, that the tree of which Adam ate was no afterthought with God. Adam's ignorance of good did not lead to its planting. It was already grown and bearing fruit. Moreover, it was not hidden in some distant corner, in an impenetrable thicket, unapproachable and forbidding. It was in the very midst of the garden, accessible, and desirable in every way. If it was simply a question of keeping Adam from eating its fruit, it could easily have been removed. Far simpler yet, it need never have been planted.

God alone was responsible for all of the accessories in Adam's transgression. It is of still greater significance that it combined in itself two inseparable functions. Perhaps we would have preferred one tree to teach the knowledge of good, and another to initiate into the knowledge of evil; but this is impossible in the very nature of things. We may strive to conceive of light apart from darkness, but it proves impossible. Light may drive out all darkness, yet its realization depends on its opposite. So good cannot be known by human beings, apart from evil.[2]

---

2. *The Problem of Evil and the Judgments of God*, pages 27-28, 34-35.

Chapter 29

"All Things Are of God"

All things are of God. — Paul, the Apostle[1]

It is sad that many professing believers seem to believe in a "god" who is somehow less than God. Our Father, the God of Scripture, is the absolute Sovereign of the universe. How could it be otherwise and He remain God? Any concept that is less than this is weighed in the balances and found lacking!

In 1885 Arthur P. Adams (1845-1925) wrote concerning Paul's powerful statement that *"all things are of God"*:

> There is *no* statement in the Bible, that was made by an apostle, that is more remarkable and even startling than this statement. When you think of it seriously, it seems as though Paul was very unguarded and careless in his language. We are apt to think that he ought to have modified and limited it in some way, such as … all GOOD things are of God.
>
> But *no*, Paul makes the sweeping, unqualified statement, *"All things are of [i.e., out of] God."* Furthermore, so im-

---
1. II Corinthians 5:18

portant did Paul consider this truth that he repeats it over and over again.

The direct statement is made no less than six times in the writings of the apostle:

> *For of Him, and through Him, and to Him, are all things.*[2]

> *There is but one God, the Father, of Whom are all things.*[3]

> *All things are of God.*[4]

> *All things are of God.*[5]

> *The purpose of Him Who works all things after the counsel of His Own will.*[6]

> *For Whom are all things, and by Whom are all things.*[7]

Now, was the apostle careless and a little too bold in these utterances, or did he mean just what he said, and are they true, taken full strength? I say, without any hesitation, yes, to the two latter questions. The more we learn (the more revelation) of God's works and ways, the more we shall understand that, in a sense, absolutely *"all things are of God."*

The knowledge that *"all things are of God"* can settle the weary heart and bring peace to the troubled mind. Regardless of the situations that we face, all things are out of God.

---

2. Romans 11:36.
3. I Corinthians 8:6.
4. I Corinthians 11:12.
5. II Corinthians 5:18.
6. Ephesians 1:11.
7. Hebrews 2:10.

The Law of Circularity

Man is born to trouble, as the sparks fly upward. — Job, from the Old Testament[8]

We all are familiar with the saying, "You only live once." The truth is that we all live *twice*. This life is only stage one of our existence. In resurrection we will experience the sequel to this life – a far grander and superior successor to this one.

This first life is hard. It is hard by the design of God.

This law is based on a simple principle. There once was nothing but God. Scriptures teach us that all things come from Him, that all things operate through Him, and that all is moving on a course back to Him.

Out of Him and through Him and into Him are all things.[9]

Here we find the simple, glorious truth in a nutshell:

(1) *All things come out of God.*
(2) *All things operate through God.*
(3) *All things move back to God.*

The knowledge that ALL is *out of God,* that ALL is *through God,* and that ALL is moving back *to God* can settle even the weariest heart and bring peace to the most troubled mind.

Father is in control.

Rest in that.

---
8. Job 5:7.
9. Romans 11:36.

Chapter 30

"All Things Work Together"

We know that all things work together for good to them who love God, to them who are the called according to His purpose. — Paul, the Apostle[1]

Regardless of what those who profess to speak for God may say, God has not been haphazardly working His way through the stages of time. He has been closely following His definite plan for the ages.

God has planned His work, and He has been working His plan - all to fulfill His Own predetermined purpose. His plan is, always has been, and always will be right on schedule - in all of its fullness.

God is actively at work in us, even in the circumstances of life that we may dread most. Do not be discouraged. Do not fret. Trust Him there. Rest fully and confidently in His work. The God Who works *"everything by the intention of His Own*

---

1. Romans 8:28.

will" finds no challenge with the circumstances and details of life – not even the hard ones. Nothing poses an obstacle to Him – after all, He *is* the Almighty God.

Therefore, there is nothing that comes our way that God does not take and make an instrument of His work in our lives. Regardless of what comes our way our Father can *work* them together for good. After all, He is the Master Workman, and we are His *Master*-piece.

Listen to the *Concordant Version's* wonderful translation of Romans 8:28.

> *Now we are aware that God is working all together for the good of those who are loving God, who are called according to the purpose.*

Paul said, *"Now we are aware …"* Are you aware? Regardless of the situations that we face, *Father is in control.*

Rest in that.

Chapter 31

THE POTTER HAS THE POWER

Has not the potter power over the clay? — Paul, the Apostle[1]

As we have noticed before, in the Scriptures our Father is spoken of as a Potter; this is an analogy that places great emphasis on His ever-present hand and well-designed plan in our lives.

The Potter always has complete power over His clay. He designs and makes His clay-creation according to His Own masterful plan. He is active in His craftsmanship with His hands-on skill.

Isaiah the Prophet also confirmed this important principle:

> O Lord, You are our Father; we are the clay, and You our Potter; and we all are the work of Your hand.[2]

Paul validates this universal principle of our Father as the Potter, and we as His clay.

---
1. Romans 9.21.
2. Isaiah 64:8.

Shall the thing formed say to Him Who formed it, "Why have You made me this way?" Has not the Potter power over the clay, of the same lump to make one vessel to honor, and another to dishonor?[3]

Down to the Potter's House

In the Old Testament book written by Jeremiah, God calls him *"down to the potter's house."*[4] It is critically important for us to *"go down to the potter's house."* It is only here that we will ever gain the true reality of the divine perspective. When Jeremiah went down to the potter's house, there he saw the potter fashioning *"a work on the wheels."*

The Potter Is in Control

Of course, Jeremiah could see the clay clearly for what it was – just passive material, and that it was the potter, and the potter ALONE, who was steady at his important work.

It was the potter who *"wrought a work on the wheels."* A visit to the potter's house reveals that it is *all* about the potter. The clay, after all, was just soil from the earth – completely powerless over its own design and destiny.

The Potter Is Responsible

Whatever is made of the clay on the potter's wheel is *totally* the responsibility of the potter. Clay does not have the power to make itself into anything. Nor does it have the power to resist the potter's purposes.

---

3. Romans 9:20-21.
4. Jeremiah 18:1-6.

Marred Vessels

The vessel that he made of clay was marred in the hand of the potter.

Jeremiah saw that the vessel was *"marred"* – but do not miss this! It was *"marred in the hand of the potter."*

Of course it was! The clay can't mar itself! If the clay vessel is *"marred,"* it is the potter's responsibility.

A trip to the potter's house will reveal the hand of the potter in everything – even in *all* of life's brokenness. After all, He is the one who mars the vessel; it is *his* doing. Clearly and simply, any vessel is what it is *because of the potter.*

Marred, but Still in the Potter's Hand

Being predestinated according to the purpose of Him Who works everything by the intention of His Own will.[5]

We are in the hand of The Potter. He is making us. Regardless of the stage of the clay's formation on the wheel, it is always in the Potter's controlling hand. Furthermore, not only is the clay on the wheel in the Potter's power, the clay is also always close to the Potter – for His hands are all over the clay. This speaks of the closeness of the Potter and His clay.

What peace we have, who truly consider these words. It matters not what our lot in life may be; what our circumstances may be like – each of His vessels rests ever secure in His able hands.

For in Him we live, and move, and have our being.[6]

---
5. Ephesians 1:11.
6. Acts 17:28.

This is the central truth that will allow us to,

Be anxious for nothing.[7]

William Mealand (1873-1957)[8] wrote of this wonderful truth.

> How great a thing it is to realize ourselves as in His Hand! What equipoise and calm! For then, should wayward circumstance, or mood's despair come near, it is to find us still within that hand. As our *"faithful Creator,"*[9] His Word is confirmed to our hearts in all its fine gradations: *"I have made, and I will bear. Even I will carry, and will deliver you."*[10]

He Made It Again – Another Vessel

He made it again another vessel, as seemed good to the potter to make it.

Jeremiah also saw a process. He saw the potter making the clay over again into another vessel. If the clay is *"made again another vessel,"* that, too, is equally and entirely the potter's responsibility. The potter is always responsible for whatever he makes.

THE *Potter* is faithful to continue His work until He has made the clay into the vessel of His Own desire and plan. This is simply the Potter's way: the clay is marred and then made new. We see it in the entire story of creation, for, there is coming a day when there will be a *"new heaven and a new earth, wherein dwells righteousness."*[11]

---

7. Philippians 4:6.
8. *In the Hand of the Potter*, in the *Unsearchable Riches Magazine*.
9. I Peter 4:19.
10. Isaiah 46:4.
11. II Peter 3:13.

The Spinning of the Potter's Wheel

Be honest, do you not often feel that your life is spinning out of control? Does it not seem to you to be quite a mess, that it is simply marred (ruined), veering wildly on a purposeless course?

This is nothing more than the spinning of the Potter's wheel beneath you.

The Pressure of the Potter's Hands

Do the pressures of life bear down hard on you? Does the pressure feel too much at times, more than you can bear?

Paul, our Apostle, felt these pressures hard. They seemed unbearable and life-ending. Listen to his heartfelt expression, that he was

> *Pressed out of measure, above strength, insomuch that we despaired even of life.*[12]

Know this truth: these are not the mere pressures of "circumstances" that you feel – this is the hand of the Potter pressing ever so firmly on the surface of your clay. Do you think that this pressure is hindering the work of the Potter in your life? No, indeed, IT *IS* the work of the Potter!

Beloved of the Potter, do not be discouraged with His loving work of wisdom. Trust Him implicitly. Patiently wait on Him as He does His life-long work on you. After all, you are His workmanship, and He alone is responsible.

Do not be disappointed with His work, His methods and His timing. Simply trust Him unreservedly. He is absolutely

---
12. II Corinthians 1:8.

skillful and faithful and He will accomplish His work (you) to supreme perfection!

"On Thy Potter's Wheel"

> Remember, Lord, Thou hast not made me good.
> Or if Thou didst, it was so long ago
> I have forgotten – and never understood,
> I humbly think. At best it was a crude,
> A rough-hewn goodness, that did need this woe,
> This sin, these harms of all kinds fierce and rude.
> To shape it out, making it live and grow.
>
> But Thou art making me, I thank Thee, Sire.
> What Thou hast done and doest Thou know'st well,
> And I will help Thee: gently in the fire
> I will lie burning; on Thy potter's wheel
> I will whirl patient, though my brain should reel.
> Thy grace shall be enough the grief to quell,
> And growing strength perfect through weakness dire.
>
> — George MacDonald (1824-1905)[13]

Do not fret. His work is larger and grander than we can see from the vantage of the spinning wheel. You *are* who you *are* because God has made you that way. You are *ever* changing – marred and remade – because He is the Potter, and you are His clay. The Potter is steadily and devotedly working His clay. He is working, making you the vessel of His Own choosing.

Shall the thing formed say to him who formed it, "Why have you made me this way?"[14]

Because you are God's clay – His *"workmanship"* – *He* is re-

---
13. *Diary of an Old Soul* (1880).
14. Romans 9:20

THE POTTER HAS THE POWER

sponsible for who you are at every stage of the process. God will use His turning wheel and the firm pressure of His hands at His Own discretion.

The Potter has power – He has power OVER the clay. Father is *always* the Potter, and we are *always* His clay.

Regardless of the situations that we face, *Father is in control.*

Rest in that.

The Conclusion of the Whole Matter

Chapter 32

BEING OK

You're never going to be OK in this life.

Regardless of what our outward appearances sometimes may seem to suggest, we *all* are very fragile and flawed. All of us are – *without a single exception*. You, along with the rest of Father's creation, have been thus subjected. No one can escape it; not even you.

In the resurrection, all of your imperfections will be gloriously and permanently corrected. For the time being, though, you might as well go ahead and admit it: you're broken, and you aren't going to be "fixed" now. You may have days that are better than others, circumstances that appear to indicate that you might be OK, but count on it – the wearisome cycle will recur.

Though you may appear to have recurring periods of better circumstances and better performances, what ultimately stops you from being truly OK will never change in your temporal life. The root of your problem is not in your varied and fluctuating circumstances; they are actually coming from the design of God found in you – the failure to which *He* has subjected you. He has purposefully and expertly created you with flaws – an abundance of them – that will never go away in this lifetime.

This is the way that Father has designed it for now. Remember that He is bringing you to a place where you are OK with not being OK, where you simply rest in His current purpose and plan in your training and development for that marvelous culmination that He has designed especially for you – in your next life. God Himself, in His great wisdom and love for you, has – at this time – subjected you to futility, and nothing will change it.

Because of this wise and competent plan of Father, the real answer is never to be found in you at all. The answer is found only in Him. It's found in knowing just Who He really is, and what His plan is for you in this current life. The solution is found in Father's abounding grace for you, even in the middle of your most trying circumstances.

Don't be discouraged when you look around. What you see is not the end of your Father's plan and purpose. You're not seeing His finished product. He is actively at work in you in every circumstance of your life. He is gradually and effectively working *"everything by the intention of His Own will,"* including your *things*. The circumstances of your life pose no challenge for Him – not even your most severe ones. *Nothing* presents an obstacle to Him, since He *is* the *Almighty* God.

Don't be overwhelmed: you're not the Workman. He is. He's the One in charge. He loves you unconditionally, and He's molding you – day-by-day – into *all* that He intends for you to be, regardless of what you think you currently see at the present.

BEING OK

One day you're going to be OK; but until then you can be OK with not being OK. It's all Father's plan. To Him, beautiful is the mess you are.

Relax, and enjoy *His* work.

Postscript

FACTS CONCERNING GOD AND YOU

All things are of God (I Corinthians 11:12).

They come out of, operate through and return back to Him (Romans 11:36). *He works everything by the intention of His Own will* (Ephesians 1:11).

God is Love (I John 4:8, 16).

He loves you greatly (Ephesians 2:4).

True love – His love – never fails (I Corinthians 13:8).

You can love Him because He first loved you (I John 4:19).

Nothing can separate you from His love (Romans 8:35-37).

You live, move and have your being in Him (Acts 17:28).

You have been made uniquely different by Him (I Corinthians 4:7).

You are what you are by His grace (I Corinthians 15:10).

You are His handiwork (Ephesians 2:10).

Your steps are ordered by Him (Psalm 37:23).

All of your days were written in His book before you were born (Psalm 139:16).

He currently has subjected you to frailty (Romans 8:20).

He is working it all for your good (Romans 8:28).

He will finish what He started in you (Philippians 1:6).

You can give Him thanks for everything (Ephesians 5:20).

Rest in these facts.

Your Part

Now that you have read this book, it's your turn.

If the truths presented here have helped you, don't let these truths die in your hands.

Please write to us and let us know your thoughts concerning its content.

Consider assisting us in getting this book into the hands of those who would be encouraged and strengthened by its message:

- Recommend it to your friends and loved ones.
- Order additional copies to give as gifts.
- Keep extra copies on hand to loan to others.

If you have not read the author's other works, order them today.

We would be honored to have your fellowship in getting this book freely to those who hunger spiritually. We have daily opportunities to send it to pastors, Sunday school teachers, Bible college professors and students, Bible class teachers, and prisoners.

Do You Subscribe to the Bible Student's Notebook™?

This is a periodical that ...
- Promotes the study of the Bible.
- Encourages the growth of the believer in grace.
- Supports the role of the family patriarch.
- Is dedicated to the recovery of truth that has too long been hidden under the veils of traditionalism, prejudice, misunderstanding and fear.
- Is not connected with any "Movement," "Organization," "Mission," or separate body of believers, but is sent forth to and for all saints.

The *Bible Student's Notebook*™ is a *free* electronic publication published weekly (52 times a year).

SUBSCRIBE TODAY!

To receive your *free* electronic subscription, email us at:
bsn@studyshelf.com

By *special order* you may also subscribe to a printed, mailed edition for only $1.00 per issue (to cover production and mailing costs). Example: ½ Year (26 issues) = $26; 1 Year (52 issues) = $52

Bible Student's Notebook™
PO Box 265 Windber, PA 15963
www.BibleStudentsNotebook.com
1-800-784-6010

DAILY EMAIL GOODIES™

Do you receive our Daily Email Goodies™?

These are free daily emails that contain short quotes, articles, and studies on Biblical themes.

These are the original writings of Clyde L. Pilkington, Jr., as well as gleanings from other authors.

Here is what our readers are saying:

"Profound! Comforting! Calming! Wonderful!" – NC

"The Daily Email Goodies continue to bless my heart! ... They provide plenty of food for thought." – IL

"I really appreciate the Goodies!" – VA

"Your Daily Email Goodies are making me aware of authors whose names I don't even know." – GA

"I am glad to be getting the Daily Email Goodies – keep 'em coming." – IN

Request to be added to our free Daily Email Goodies™

If you would like to be added to the mailing list, email us at:
<u>Goodies@StudyShelf.com</u>

MORE BOOKS BY:
Clyde L. Pilkington, Jr

Believer's Warfare, The: Wearing the Armor of Light in the Darkness of this World

(#7000) The believer is in the middle of an ancient spiritual warfare that is as old as mankind. The battle itself, although intense, is not complicated. It is not a process of spiritual hoop-jumping. Indeed it is simple. The Believer's Warfare surveys a few key passages of Scripture to reveal God's sure plan of victory in the life of His saints. – 48 pp., BK.

Bible Student's Notebook, The (VOLUMES)

The Bible Student's Notebook is a periodical dedicated to the: - Promotion of Bible study - Encouragement of the believer's growth in grace - Support of the role of family patriarch - Recovery of truth that has too long been hidden under the veils of traditionalism, prejudice, misunderstanding and fear. The Bible Student's Notebook is not connected with any "Church," "Movement," "Organization," "Society," "Mission," or separate body of believers, but is sent forth to and for all of God's saints. Available in Paperback Volumes.

Being OK with Not Being OK: Embracing God's Design for You – and Everyone You Know (and Don't Know)

(#1985) For now, you're broken, and you aren't going to be "fixed." Granted, you may have some days that are better than others, some circumstances that seem to indicate that you are "OK," but the wearisome cycle simply will recur.

Thus it is by design – by divine design. Father is bringing you to a place where you are OK with not being OK, where you simply rest in His current purpose and plan in your training and development for that grand and magnificent culmination that He has so wonderfully and skillfully designed especially for you – in your next life. – 134 pp., PB.

Church in Ruins, The: Brief Thoughts on II Timothy

(#3325) This brief survey of Paul's last epistle will reveal that, while almost 2000 years have transpired, the condition of the church has remained the same, and indeed has worsened in accordance with Paul's warning to Timothy. This book is not a call for a re-awakening of "the church," because it is apparent that this is not Father's plan. Rather, it is a call to individual men – men whose place in the Christian religious system has left them empty, stagnant and restless – to awaken to Father's call to be His faithful servant and stand outside of that system to look for other faithful men as well. – 128 pp., PB.

Daily Goodies: 365 Thoughts on Scriptural Truths

(#1747) This is a great resource for personal and family study, as well as a valuable reference volume covering many varied biblical themes. This is a collection of choice selections from the author's Daily E-mail Goodies. These free daily e-mails began being issued in 2003 and contain studies on scriptural themes. – 490 pp., PB. *$19.^{95}*

Daily Gleanings – 365 Selections on Scriptural Truths

(#1836) This book contains a collection of gleanings from some 200 different authors. These excerpts are intended to be an encouragement to those who are walking on a different path with the Lord – a journey that is *"outside of the camp."*

Some quotations are from beloved and trusted authors, but more often than not, they are from unusual sources. Sometimes, it is simply amazing how an author can admit in print to some grand truth that their writings and ministries otherwise generally deny. For the authors of these quotes, the truth that is conveyed by them may oddly seem "out of place"; but in some ways, the more unlikely the source, the more amazingly it testifies to the truth – and the fact that it cannot be hidden. – 253 pp., PB. *$19.^{95}*

I Choose! Living Life to Its Fullest

(#4120) Forty-Eight Daily Thoughts on Divine Life. You are alive! Yet not just alive, but alive with the very life of God! Don't allow your "What if ..." imaginations of the past or the future to lay claim to the present that God has given you. Allow the objective, unchanging truth of who God has made you in the Lord Jesus Christ to transform your mind and life as you take this spiritual journey of "I Choose." – 192 pp., PB.

Due Benevolence: A Study of Biblical Sexuality

(#3775) Think you have read all that there is on the subject of sexuality from the Bible? Think again! Religious moralists have taken the wonderful gifts of human beauty and sexuality, and made them something dirty and sinful. Much is at stake regarding truth, as well as the nature and character of God Himself. A groundbreaking work providing:

- A refreshingly honest and uninhibited look at sexuality.
- A breath of fresh air from the religious and Victorian mentality.
- A daring and valuable glimpse at the wonderful light just outside sexuality's prison-cell door.

– 220 pp., PB.

God's Holy Nation: Israel and Her Earthly Purpose (Contrasted with the Body of Christ and Its Heavenly Purpose)

(#2275) Israel plays a key role in God's plan of the ages. Though currently she has been set aside "until the times of the nations be fulfilled," He is by no means done with her.

Today, God is operating His purpose in the ecclesia – the Church, the Body of Christ. The Scriptures provide us with the clear, critical distinction between God's earthly nation and Christ's celestial body.

Christendom, however, has diminished Israel's divine significance in an attempt to advance their artificial homogenization of Scripture's grand theme, thus obscuring the glorious evangel of our day – "the Good News of the Happy God" committed to the trust of Paul, our Apostle.

This work highlights some of the more prominent distinctions which belong to God's literal, physical, earthly nation. In so doing, it is our desire to allow the reader to see more clearly God's dealings with God's favored nation, so that they may in turn embrace a far greater calling and purpose. – 360 pp., PB.

King James Version, The – 400 Years of Bondage – 1611-2011

(#4682) 1611 was not a high spiritual mark in the history of the church, the Body of Christ. Instead of being a grand year of the pinnacle of preservation or perfection of God's Word, it was rather the sad depths of the subtle corrupting of God's Word by the historic union of governmental and ecclesiastical politics. – 72 pp., PB. *$9.^{25}*

Heaven's Embassy: The Divine Plan & Purpose of the Home

(#5675) The home is central to all of God's dealings with man throughout the course of time. It is His Divine "institution" and "organization" upon the earth, and for the believer, it is the Embassy of Heaven. An embassy is "the residence or office of an ambassador." Since the believer is an ambassador of the Lord Jesus Christ (II Corinthians 5:14-21), his home is thus the Divine Embassy of heavenly ministry. Pauline ministry is centered in the homes of believers. This is even the true sphere of the Body of Christ; for this reason our apostle speaks of "church in thy house." This book doesn't focus upon the external specifics of the ministry of Heaven's Embassy (such as hospitality); that will be saved for another volume. Instead, it looks at the inner-workings of the Embassy itself; focusing upon its very nature and internal purpose and function. – 250 pp., PB.

I Am! Who and What God Says I Am! The Divine Reckoning of the Renewed Mind; Daily Thoughts on Divine Life

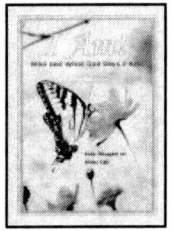

(#1737) People are always talking about their attempts to discover their true selves – of trying to "find themselves." The believer in the Lord Jesus Christ needs to find out who they *really* are. This doesn't need to be such a difficult search. All that is really needed is a careful look at the Scriptures, and a simple faith in the words of who and what God says we are. God knows who we are; all we need to do is to *believe Him.* This book catalogs the Divine Record of who and what God says that you are. It is a short encyclopedia of faith – the truth about you. It is the truth about you, simply because it is *God* Who has said it. God has spoken these truths concerning you – the *real* you. Believe His record! Refuse to be the shell of a person, pushed into a mold of Adamic conformity. Be the real you that God has uniquely designed you to be. Refuse to be bullied out of your divinely designed identity that our Father has given you. – 107 pp., PB. *$9.^{95}*

Nothing Will Be Lost! The Truth About God's Good News

(#3750) This is an abridgement of the larger work The Salvation of All. It is designed as a give-away edition, with quantity pricing available. – 88 pp., PB.

Outsiders, The: God's Called-Out Ones – A Biblical Look at the Church – God's Ecclesia

(#4125) In 1995, after sixteen years of being in the "pastorate" the author walked away. He left the "religious system" by resigning from the very "church" and "ministry" he had formed. In many ways this work is a testament to these actions. This testimony was thirty years in the making – the results of a spiritual journey that the author found to be common to other saints scattered throughout the world and across history. This is an opportunity to explain why some who love the Lord no longer "go to church." It does not seek to persuade others to do something different; but rather to be simply who and what they already are "in Him." This is an uncovering of the truth of the church, and an encouragement for the members of His Body to enjoy the position and standing "in Christ" that they already possess, realizing that they are truly *"complete in Him"* (Colossians 2:10), that He alone is their Life (Colossians 3:4), and that His Life is full of freedom (Galatians 5:1). – 128 pp., PB.

Plowboy's Bible, The: God's Word for Common Man

(#4425) Shocking conclusions from the man that brought you The King James Bible Song. This book represents years of study and a significant change in understanding. Raised on and trained in a "King James Only" position, most of the author's teaching ministry was centered on the defense of the KJV. He had early associations with major proponents of this position and their followers. He actively taught classes and seminars on the subject of Bible versions. For many years he distributed thousands of books from a collection of over 100 different titles in support of the KJV position. Here he shares what he has come to see that has caused him to completely abandon his former position. – 254 pp., PB.

Salvation Of ALL, The: Creation's Final Destination (A Biblical Look at Universal Reconciliation)

(#7001) The Gospel of our Lord and Savior, Jesus Christ is truly better "Good News" than we could ever have imagined. It is far more glorious than religion would ever have us believe. The Salvation of All is a book about a "Good News" that will reach its final goal in the salvation of all mankind. – 302 pp., PB.

Suffering: God's Forgotten Gift

Two gifts given to the believer are mentioned by Paul in Philippians 1:29. The first is *"to believe on Him."* This is a glorious gift. Every believer has been given this gift from God. Those who possess it may not even fully recognize it as a gift from Him, but indeed faith is God's wonderful gift to us. Faith is a rich gift from God, but there is also another gift from God to the believer mentioned by Paul in Philippians 1:29 that is equally as glorious. The second gift is *"also to suffer for His sake."* This, too, is a glorious gift. Every believer has been given this gift from God as well, but those who possess it often do not fully recognize it for what it is. Indeed, suffering for His sake similarly is God's wonderful gift to us. Paul teaches us to embrace this second gift as well as we do the first! – 100 pp., PB.

World Affairs and National Politics – and the High Calling of God in Christ Jesus

(#4250) When did nationalism begin? What is God's purpose for nationalism? Is the United States a Christian nation? Does any government have Favored Nation Status with God today? Should believers support Israel? What did Paul have to say about our citizenship? What is our role in relation to nations? Is our job to rid the world of evil? What should the believer's attitude be toward earthly authority? Should all obedience to earthly magistrates be absolute? Are believers to pay their taxes? Where does voting and jury duty fit in? Why was the apostle Paul executed? These and many other questions are addressed in this groundbreaking work! – 258 pp., PB. *$14.^{95}*

To Order:

visit: ClydePilkington.com
or
call Toll Free: 1-800-784-6010

ENJOY BOOKS?

Visit us at:

www.StudyShelf.com

Over the years we have often been asked to recommend books. The requests come from believers who longed for material with substance. Study Shelf™ is a collection of books which are, in our opinion, the very best in print. Many of these books are "unknown" to the members of the Body of Christ at large, and most are not available at your local "Christian" bookstore.

YOU CAN:

Read

A wealth of articles from past issues of the *Bible Student's Notebook* ™

Purchase

Rare and hard to find books, booklets, leaflets, Bibles, etc. in our 24/7 online store.

CPSIA information can be obtained
at www.ICGtesting.com
Printed in the USA
FFOW02n0415010714
6117FF